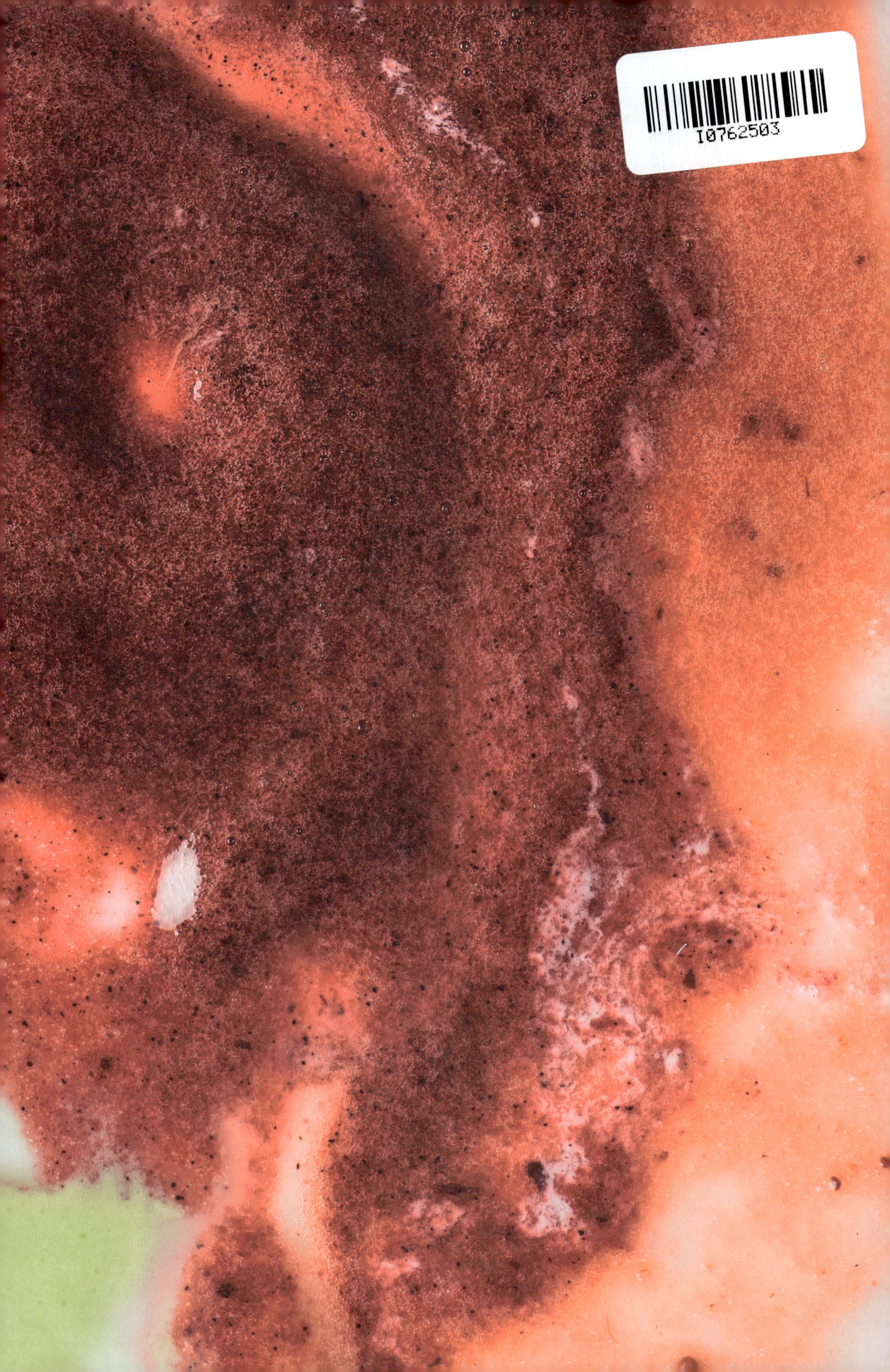
I0762503

THE ART OF FROZEN DESSERTS

EMMANUEL RYON

THE ART OF FROZEN DESSERTS

tra.publishing

CONTENTS

PREFACE

EMMANUEL RYON

MEILLEUR OUVRIER DE FRANCE GLACIER
(BEST CRAFTSMAN IN FRANCE, ICE CREAM)
WORLD PASTRY CHAMPION

I'm truly excited to share my frozen world with you. Through this book, I want to pass on my passion for ice creams and sorbets. Flavors, textures, and colors are what keep me moving forward each day. These three are the pillars of my creativity. But one more element, perhaps the most important, guides it all: pleasure.

The pleasure of indulging is what drives me to explore new paths, test new flavor combinations, and invent new textures. I love blending the skills of an ice cream maker with those of a pastry chef, two crafts that mean a great deal to me.

One of my greatest sources of inspiration is my daughter, Marie-Lou, who is the other sweet tooth in the family. She has an amazing palate, and we often do blind tastings together for fun. She surprises me every time and inspires me deeply in what I create.

I have been thinking about writing a new book on ice cream and sorbet for a long time. I never quite had the time to follow through, but now, here it is. I'm thrilled to finally bring it to life.

I hope you enjoy discovering my world.

FOREWORD

ANNE-SOPHIE PIC

I first met Emmanuel Ryon over ten years ago. We exchanged ideas for a while about pastry creation.

I really enjoyed those conversations and introducing each other to our favorite ingredients. For me, it was rose geranium and matcha tea. For him, turmeric and black lemon.

Frozen desserts have always been at the heart of Emmanuel's work. He's a true master of the craft, and it's become his signature. It's a passion I share as well, since I often use ice cream to enhance my dishes.

In many ways, ice cream is like a sauce for a chef. It becomes part of their signature, tying all the ingredients together. These days, the line between savory cooking and pastry is incredibly thin. Dishes can be elevated with a touch of ice cream, and desserts can incorporate savory notes like roots and vegetables.

Ice cream is also about color and texture. It reflects evolving trends in pastry, drawing on unconventional ingredients like flowers, spices, and teas. It can be smooth or chewy, bitter, or spicy. Its range of textures and flavors is vast, making it a never-ending source of inspiration.

Letting ice cream melt just a little helps it reveal its fullness, its aromas, and how it connects with the ingredients around it. I love Emmanuel's approach, creating ice cream that is feminine, sensual, and bold in its flavor pairings.

With this book, Emmanuel Ryon shines a spotlight on ice cream as a central part of indulgence. He makes it approachable with recipes that are easy to follow, and he encourages everyone to embrace the art of frozen desserts.

FOREWORD

PIERRE HERMÉ

Chilled, frosty, full of flair—that's the kind of ice cream you'll find in this book by Emmanuel Ryon, a master of the frozen arts. His signature lies in shaping texture, creaminess, fluidity, and bold flavor to create one-of-a-kind desserts.

I have great admiration and deep respect for Emmanuel's work. I've known him for many years, and his creativity shows not only in form but also in the bold taste profiles of his creations, where texture always plays a central role.

A top-tier pastry professional and *Meilleur Ouvrier de France glacier* since the early 2000s, Emmanuel has brought an entirely fresh perspective to the world of ice cream. With his longtime friend and business partner, Olivier Ménard, he opened Une Glace à Paris to showcase every facet of the full spectrum of ice creams and modern pastry, with quality and flavor as the guiding principles.

He's a creative risk-taker, uniting ice cream making with a modern, reimagined French pastry style. He focuses deeply on textures and their contrasts; that's how he approaches flavor. His hot-cold *Galette des Rois* is a striking example of his originality and fearless innovation.

Alongside timeless classics, Emmanuel crafts forward-thinking creations like his Jerusalem artichoke ice cream with artichoke chips or his frozen tomato with tomato-basil sorbet, both of which are shared in this book.

His delightful Frenchies, a marshmallow-wrapped ice cream, and his travel cakes blend the worlds of pastry and frozen desserts in a way that sets him apart.

After a first book written for professionals, I'm proud to introduce this new one made for everyone. It's a way to recognize Emmanuel's incredible dedication and skill. With a touch of extravagance, he elevates ice cream to an art form.

INTRODUCTION

JOURNEY OF A PASSIONATE ARTISAN

Emmanuel Ryon's love affair with ice cream began, like all culinary journeys, with a spark, a moment of revelation. It happened when he tasted the ice creams of Bernardd Huguet, who at the time held the title of *Meilleur Ouvrier de France* for ice cream. Emmanuel found them extraordinary. That was when he first understood the power of perfect texture in frozen desserts. Trained as a pastry chef, he shifted course and stepped into the world of ice cream.

THE BIRTH OF A PASSION

Emmanuel is a discreet and humble man. He doesn't talk much about himself and rarely opens up. What we do know is that he's a meticulous worker, a tireless dreamer, and someone with deep resolve. People often say he's both traditional and modern. But the moment he starts talking about ice cream—how to handle it, what he loves experimenting with, the level of excellence he hopes it will one day be known for—he becomes animated and enthusiastic. He's known for daring to explore unexpected flavors like beet, turmeric, and carrot, inspired by his travels abroad or simply by his own curiosity.

Emmanuel says he fell into pastry by default. Born in Bourg-en-Bresse, France, he grew up surrounded by cooking and especially baking. His passion was rooted in family: a mother who cooked, a grandmother who made every possible dessert for family gatherings, and an uncle who owned a pastry shop in Ferney-Voltaire, all of which laid the groundwork for his future calling.

As a child, he would rush home just to bake cakes. At fourteen, instead of pursuing lengthy academic studies, he chose the hands-on path of apprenticeship.

After earning his pastry certification, he was fortunate to work with, and choose, mentors who taught him precision, creativity, speed, and endurance. He started with Gabriel Paillasson, who instilled in him a love for competitions. Later, he joined the famed Belgian La Maison Wittamer, where he honed his skills in chocolate. Then at Philippe Segond's Riederer pastry shop in Aix-en-Provence, he discovered that pastry could be reimagined. He learned to break the rules and invent new ones, developing a unique aesthetic vision that opened creative doors he hadn't considered before. These early experiences helped him shape a personal style fueled by boundless passion.

Although his career path may seem similar to many other chefs at first glance, Emmanuel's story stands apart. He entered twenty-six competitions and won most of them. Each one brought a new challenge and ultimately unlocked his creativity. He reached two major milestones back to back: in 1999, he was named World Pastry Champion; and in 2000, he was awarded the prestigious title of *Meilleur Ouvrier de France* in ice cream. These two years, full of emotion and sacrifice, were driven by one thing: his love for ice cream.

These titles opened the door to another dream: to travel and discover the world. When Bellouet School offered him a chance to teach professionals abroad, lead demonstrations, and write a book about ice cream, he seized it.

une Glace à Paris
Emmanuel Ryon

As his reputation grew, he met Andrey Dellos, the founder of the renowned Café Pouchkine and several high-end restaurants in Moscow, Paris, and New York. Emmanuel collaborated with him for more than a decade. "I had to create everything from scratch. The only instruction was to design the best pastry in the world," he recalls modestly. This partnership became a fertile exchange of ideas focused on creating desserts that felt almost dreamlike. He later teamed up with Chef Anne-Sophie Pic and her restaurants, launched Le Frank restaurant at the Louis Vuitton Foundation in 2014, and simultaneously pursued an old dream: opening his own ice cream parlor. That dream came true in 2015 when he joined forces with his friend Olivier Ménard to open Une Glace à Paris in the heart of the historic Marais district.

His journey and creative world are the result of long-held dreams brought to life, shaped by determination and a desire to carve his own path. That's where the true uniqueness of Emmanuel lies. He lives, dreams, and thrives for the love of ice cream.

FOR THE LOVE OF ICE CREAM

Few things bring Emmanuel more joy than ice cream. A true gourmand, he first develops it to please himself. When asked how he feels when he eats one of his own creations, he doesn't hesitate: "It brings me immense joy," he says.

Being an ice cream maker is demanding, but that suits him just fine. He enjoys working with the product, the process, and the technology. He uses every resource available, constantly reinventing himself to elevate this art form. For him, excellence in ice cream lies in its almost alchemical transformation.

He's driven by the desire to craft refined, elegant ice creams with unexpected flavors. He explores new textures that unfold and evolve in the mouth. Although he doesn't claim to have invented anything, he strives to reimagine traditional desserts and classic frozen treats with a fresh perspective.

His ice creams and sorbets are rich, balanced, and full of flavor. His sorbets stand out for their high fruit content rather than added flavorings. Most of the fruit he uses is purchased fresh and then turned into purée. Focused on authentic taste and texture, Emmanuel avoids all synthetic additives such as artificial flavors, enhancers, or preservatives. His ice creams are also low in egg content. The result is ice cream that feels smooth on the palate, yet is structurally sound enough to hold its form.

It's all made possible by meticulous work on texture. Emmanuel believes that the first experience of flavor comes from how something feels in the mouth, whether crispy, creamy, or smooth. That textural harmony is key to his success.

Over time, his vision continues to evolve. Powered by technical mastery, his relentless pursuit of texture quality is part of a broader mission: to restore ice cream's standing as a noble culinary art. His dream is to make ice cream a product of excellence that's accessible to all.

RESPECT FOR CREAM

Emmanuel has traveled the world. He draws inspiration from his journeys, especially in Asia and Africa, where he discovers new ingredients and spices, explores new pairings and flavors, and expands the creative scope that defines his unique take on ice cream today. On average, he visits about ten countries each year, and, during his travels, he has come to a clear conclusion: good ice cream is surprisingly rare across the globe. This realization has only deepened his commitment to excellence.

For the past thirty years, he has dedicated his life to restoring ice cream to its rightful place in both French and international gastronomy. Ice cream is certainly about indulgence, but for him, it is much more than that. It is a noble product that deserves the same respect as any fine culinary creation. It offers an incredible space for creative freedom and endless reinvention. Today, ice cream is recognized as an art form and enjoyed around the world. But in the late 1990s, it had fallen out of favor in France. Emmanuel remembers that twenty-five or thirty years ago, nearly every pastry shop in France carried a variety of frozen desserts. The most familiar and classic was the vacherin. Yet by the early 2000s, these frozen desserts—domes, vacherins, profiteroles, baked Alaskas, bombes, or yule logs—had all but vanished from pastry displays.

For Emmanuel, this disappearance cannot be attributed solely to shifts in lifestyle or changing tastes among dessert lovers. He believes it had more to do with how pastry chefs came to view ice cream itself. In his view, ice cream had been neglected, seen as something less refined. He often says that being an ice cream maker requires a level of precision and discipline that sets it apart. "It's a craft that demands rigor. It's very different from being a pastry chef or chocolatier. A pastry chef can take his time. A chocolatier can take even more time. But an ice cream maker needs to move quickly and stay sharp."

Emmanuel excels in all three disciplines: pastry, chocolate, and ice cream. His reputation, the respect of his peers, and his many collaborations with top culinary institutions, both past and present, have only strengthened his resolve to keep going. Like a true alchemist, he is one of the very few *Meilleurs Ouvriers de France* in ice cream, practicing the craft at its highest level. Through his creations and influence, he has helped bring ice cream and frozen desserts back into the spotlight of both French and international cuisine.

ICE CREAM: A MILLENNIA-OLD STORY

Everyone loves ice cream...or nearly everyone. It's enjoyed at any age, in every season, and fits almost any occasion, from family dinners and afternoon snacks to street food cravings and spontaneous indulgences. Ice cream conjures a rare kind of emotion, one that evokes joy from childhood well into adulthood. As both a dessert and a delight, it has enchanted humankind for centuries. The story of how it came to be, closely tied to the evolution of preservation methods, is nothing short of epic. And the role it has played across civilizations continues to evolve. Cultural cross-pollination, the development and transmission of artisanal skills, technological advances in refrigeration, and an ever-growing understanding of flavor balance and texture have all come together to make ice cream the enduring delight we know today.

A WELL-KEPT SECRET: FROM ANTIQUITY TO THE 17TH CENTURY

The story of ice cream, now one of the most widely consumed foods in the world, unfolds over the course of centuries. It is deeply tied to the long history of transcontinental trade and cultural exchange, but its origins remain somewhat mysterious. While many historians agree that the earliest frozen dessert recipes came from East Asia, the exact timeline is still uncertain. Everything we know about ice cream before the seventeenth century is based on hypotheses, or even what some consider poetic legends.

One story says it all began in China more than three thousand years ago. A street vendor, after a freezing night, discovered that his beverages had turned to ice. He added goat's milk and honey, and in doing so, created what may have been the first version of ice cream. This tale suggests that the Chinese knew how to prepare frozen drinks and desserts from the earliest days of their civilization.

The first recorded mention of a frozen dessert appears much later, around 500 B.C.E., describing Persian nobility enjoying a frozen dish made with snow and mashed fruits. This could have been the ancestor of *faloodeh,* a chilled dessert made with rice noodles, fruit, honey, rosewater, lemon juice, and saffron. It's possible that sugar was included even then, as King Darius the Great extended his empire to the eastern banks of the Indus River where sugarcane was already being processed. At that time, sugar was unknown outside Asia. Although Alexander the Great's conquests in the fourth century B.C.E. introduced the Greeks to sugarcane (described as "a reed that produces honey without bees"), it wasn't until the seventh century A.D. that sugarcane cultivation reached the Mediterranean region via the Arab-Muslim expansion. From there, sugar gradually made its way into Western Europe, thanks to the Crusaders, and then spread across the world.

The French word *sorbet* actually comes from Persia, where *sharbat* meant "beverage" and referred to a fruit juice chilled with snow or ice. This refreshing treat was essentially a kind of early granita or fruit ice.

In ancient Greece, as early as the fifth or fourth century B.C.E., Hippocrates—the father of medicine—recommended a mix of snow, honey, and fruit to his patients. He claimed it "revived the juices of life and promoted well-being." A few decades later, Alexander the Great was said to enjoy a similar preparation: a medley of fruit and honey kept cool in earthen pots surrounded by snow.

"The Crusaders, especially the Knights Templar, rediscovered sorbet in the Middle East during the early twelfth century."

Over time, sorbets became popular among the Roman elite. During the early days of the Roman Empire, Emperor Nero reportedly had snow transported from the Sabine Mountains and the Abruzzo region to chill his favorite treats.

From China to Persia and from ancient Greece to Rome, frozen desserts won over the great civilizations of antiquity. While the basic ingredients and freezing methods varied based on available resources, particularly spices, the techniques remained surprisingly similar. But after the fall of the Roman Empire, this rare and luxurious indulgence disappeared from Western Europe for nearly a thousand years. Meanwhile, ice-based desserts were still appreciated in the medieval Arab world.

It was the Crusaders, especially the Knights Templar, who reintroduced the Middle East's frozen treats to Europe in the twelfth century. Then, at the end of the following century, Marco Polo brought back the technique for making artificial ice after his travels through China. Having left Venice in 1271 at the age of seventeen with his father Niccolò and uncle Matteo, Polo traveled the Silk Road, passed through Acre, Persia, and Central Asia, and eventually reached Cambaluc (modern-day Beijing). There, the family was received at the court of Kublai Khan, the powerful Mongol emperor. Marco Polo remained in his service for sixteen years, fulfilling various diplomatic missions. In *The Travels of Marco Polo*, also known as *The Book of Wonders*, he described how frozen desserts were made by pouring a mixture of snow and saltpeter around barrels of syrup. Just as salt raises the boiling point of water, saltpeter lowers the freezing point below zero. This process, known since ancient times, was essentially a prototype of the modern ice cream maker. Sorbet regained popularity in Venice and at the royal courts of Italy, including the papal court in Rome.

That fruit-ice recipe likely served as the foundation for frozen desserts all the way through the Renaissance. But in the sixteenth century, a new development began: the addition of milk and sugar, which paved the way for what we now call ice cream. It was during this time that milk-based frozen desserts, like the classic Italian gelato, began to make their way across the Alps. In France, it's often said that Catherine de Medici, a Florentine noblewoman and relative of multiple popes, introduced ice cream when she married the future King Henry II in 1533 to soon become Queen of France.

However, this version of history is not fully confirmed. According to culinary historian Pierre Leclercq of the University of Liège, "Frozen drinks only began to appear in Italy in the second half of the sixteenth century, eventually becoming a true local specialty. Mixtures of snow with flavored water or wine spread throughout the peninsula, reaching even the working classes." He firmly disputes the traditional narrative. "Based on the historical evidence," he argues, "there's no reason to believe that Catherine de Medici popularized ice cream in France. First, there is no proof that Italians even knew how to make ice cream during the first half of the sixteenth century. And second, it's clear that by 1660, a century later, this technique was still unknown in Paris." Leclercq believes the story of Catherine de Medici and ice cream is a legend born in the nineteenth century, probably from *The Physiology of Taste* (1825) by Jean Anthelme Brillat-Savarin, who credited the Florentine queen with bringing the frozen dessert to France.

Whatever the case, it is well documented that by the second half of the seventeenth century, both sorbets and milk-based ice creams were served at the court of Louis XIV. Other records show that European courts were discovering and embracing this refined pleasure. In England, where ice cream appeared around the same time as in Italy, it was reportedly a regular feature at the table of Charles I during the first half of the 1600s.

"Ice cream is exquisite. What a pity it's not illegal."

A DELICACY FIT FOR ROYALTY, FROM THE PALACE TO THE STREET

In the seventeenth century, ice cream was a royal indulgence, both expensive and rare. Beyond the cost of ingredients, such as fruit, honey, and spices, came the high price of transporting snow and managing preservation methods. This era saw the rapid development of icehouses: stone- or brick-lined pits, often built partially underground, packed in winter with natural ice from ponds or basins and either crushed or compacted snow. These ice stores preserved their contents well into the height of summer and served as early cold rooms. At Versailles, the château grounds had thirteen icehouses by 1688, most of them built at the initiative of Louis XIV. They remained in use beyond the end of the Ancien Régime. The King's icehouses supplied ice year-round to the royal kitchens and those serving the queen, ministers, and other members of the court. As icehouses became more common, these benefits gradually extended to innkeepers, lemonade vendors, café owners, dairy merchants, and perfumers throughout the city, especially as public icehouses became more common.

The French writer Stendhal, in his *Italian Chronicles* (published in 1855), recounts a story from seventeenth-century Italy in which a princess, savoring an ice cream on a hot evening, exclaimed, "What a pity this isn't a sin!" In the eighteenth century, Voltaire was said to have remarked, "Ice cream is exquisite. What a pity it's not illegal." These sentiments reflect a broader shift that occurred in France, where the rise in icehouses made frozen treats more accessible. So significant was this growth that by 1701, the king issued a royal decree regulating the trade and distribution of snow and ice. Even more pivotal was the creation, in 1676, of the guild of lemonade vendors, who were granted the right to prepare and sell ices and chilled drinks. They were also authorized to distill and serve liqueurs, coffee, tea, and hot chocolate, beverages introduced only a few decades earlier that were now wildly popular in aristocratic circles.

The now-familiar phrase *café-glacier* (or ice cream parlor) has its roots in Paris at the end of the seventeenth century, thanks to a Sicilian lemonade and spirits vendor named Francesco Procopio dei Coltelli, naturalized as François Procope in 1684. In 1686, he founded the legendary Café Procope. At a time when coffee was sold from small stalls or private coffee houses (it had only reached the French capital in 1657), Procope opened an elegant establishment. With tasteful furnishings and luxurious decor, it became the first real Parisian café. His early clientele included players from a nearby tennis court, passersby in the bustling Saint-Germain district, and soon, actors from the Comédie-Française, whose new theater opened just across the street in 1689.

Before long, writers, novelists, and intellectuals gathered there, along with the fashionable elite of Paris. Café Procope quickly became both a literary and political hub. Throughout the eighteenth century, the café welcomed the likes of Montesquieu, Voltaire, Rousseau, and Diderot, and later the revolutionaries Danton, Robespierre, Desmoulins, and Marat.

In addition to coffee, spirits, and spiced wines, Procope served sorbets, chilled jellies, and ices made from fruits and flowers: flavors that urban gourmets had never encountered before. His son Alexandre carried on this tradition, and their successors continued innovating. It is said that Café Procope developed up to eighty different ice cream recipes. What was once a luxury reserved for the aristocracy was now finding its way to a broader public: an affluent bourgeoisie who gathered in cafés.

While Procope helped establish ice cream culture in Paris, the trend was gaining ground across major European cities and soon reached the shores of North America. By the mid-eighteenth century, ice cream was already being enjoyed in colonial America. A guest of the Maryland governor mentioned it in a letter as early as 1744. In the 1770s, Italian immigrant Giovanni Bosio opened the first ice cream shop in New York. And in the *New York Gazette* on May 12, 1777, an advertisement praised the French, English, Italian, and German frozen delicacies of confectioner Philip Lenzi, newly arrived from London. During his stay in Paris from 1785 to 1789 as U.S. Minister to France, Thomas Jefferson tasted ice cream and brought the recipe back with him. When he became president (1801 to 1809), he famously served ice cream to his guests at the White House.

By the early nineteenth century, American entrepreneurs and merchants were seizing the opportunity to build a lucrative ice trade, supplying ice blocks for refrigeration. One of the earliest and most notable was Frederic Tudor of Boston, who founded the Tudor Ice Company in the 1820s. He harvested ice from ponds in Massachusetts and New England and transported it by rail or ship to major nearby cities, the southern states, and destinations as far away as the Caribbean, South America, India, China, and England. This earned him the nickname "Ice King." Another pioneer, Jacob Fussell, a milk dealer in Baltimore, launched the first industrial ice cream factory in 1851.

From the courts of kings in the late 1600s to the storefronts of bustling city streets in the 1800s, ice cream had completed a remarkable journey. An entire economic sector emerged, and frozen desserts continued to grow in popularity alongside the technological advances of the Industrial Revolution. By the early twentieth century, ice cream production was booming, with large-scale factories and the rise of ice cream street vendors becoming part of everyday life.

THREE CENTURIES OF INNOVATION IN SERVICE OF ICE CREAM

Since ancient times, the biggest challenge in making ice cream and frozen treats has been mastering freezing and preservation techniques. The development of ice pits and icehouses, their widespread installation, and the organized distribution of ice are all testaments to that. From the seventeenth to the twentieth century, ice production and frozen desserts advanced in tandem. Early food literature focused more on methods of freezing and storage than on the actual recipes.

During the reign of Louis XV, Joseph Menon published one of the first collections of frozen dessert recipes in his 1750 work *La Science du maître d'hôtel confiseur.* Nearly thirty recipes appear in the chapter titled "On Ice Creams: For Freezing All Kinds of Fruit and Liquors," along with frozen fruit, iced cannelloni, and frozen cheese recipes.

In 1768, a civil servant named Emy published the first book entirely devoted to ice cream: *The Art of Properly Making Pantry Ice Creams; or The True Principles for Freezing All Refreshments (L'Art de bien faire les glaces d'office; ou Les Vrais Principes pour congeler tous les rafraîchissements).* The book outlined how to prepare various mixtures, freeze them, shape them into fruit or cannelloni, and make a wide array of frozen specialties, including iced cheeses. With a section on mousses, the work reads like a combination of a physics manual, a practical guide with tricks and tools of the trade, and a full recipe book. Over a hundred pages detail an extraordinary variety of frozen treats with flavors and ingredients that were rare or exceptional at the time: creams, fruits, prized citrus, exotic spices, coffee, chocolate, tea, vanilla, almonds, walnuts, pistachios, candied fruits, chestnuts, and liqueurs. Emy included a recipe for a cream-based ice cream made from cooked cream, first evaporating the whey, then thickening it with egg yolks or whites. The result, he wrote, was "like frozen butter—rich, smooth, and delicate...the most perfect thing."

Gradually, ice cream evolved beyond its original purpose of simply transforming fruit. The process became more complex, integrating eggs, cream, and other ingredients. While the early recipes were passed on orally, this new generation of frozen desserts was now memorialized with detailed written instructions by culinary authors.

"You'll get ice creams that resemble frozen butter: rich, smooth, and delicate...it's the most perfect thing."

Mechanizing ice cream production was the next step in making it available to a wider public. In 1843, American inventor Nancy Johnson created the first hand-cranked ice cream machine. About twenty years later, French engineer Ferdinand Carré, known for his work on refrigeration, designed a continuous ice-making machine that was showcased at the 1862 World's Fair in London. It was quickly adopted by breweries. Meanwhile, his rival, Charles Tellier, developed the first refrigeration machine.

Major technological breakthroughs followed, including low-temperature refrigeration units, freezers, and automatic churns, which transformed the entire production chain. These advances gave birth to a true cold industry. Engineers focused on texture and product quality, introducing techniques like pasteurization (patented in 1865) and high-pressure milk homogenization (invented by Auguste Gaulin in 1899). Others dreamed up new ways to enjoy ice cream. The first ice cream cones appeared at the 1904 World's Fair in St. Louis, Missouri. The chocolate-coated ice cream bar on a stick was patented by Christian Nelson in 1919. Other frozen treats on sticks or in cones soon followed, making ice cream easy to enjoy anywhere, whether on the go or at the table, and accessible to all.

The twentieth century marked the golden age of ice cream, which became a major part of the food industry. With countless variations, ice cream was now available to people from all walks of life and became a household staple around the globe.

Once a product made only in winter, ice cream is now a must-have in summer. From Italian gelato and American sundaes to French-style ice cream and fruit sorbets, frozen desserts are a universal pleasure. In France especially, ice cream has earned its place among culinary traditions. The country now ranks among the most demanding in the world when it comes to food safety and flavor quality, so unsurprisingly France has churned out high-quality and delicious desserts. The French truly love their ice cream.

CHEF'S ADVICE FOR BEGINNERS

The equipment you need to start making ice cream and sorbet at home is fairly simple, but there's one thing you absolutely need: an ice cream maker.

RECOMMENDED BASIC EQUIPMENT

1 ice cream maker

1 precision scale (accurate to the gram)

1 immersion blender

1 whisk

1 rubber spatula

1 ice cream scoop

1 probe thermometer

1 chinois or fine mesh strainer

1 stand mixer or electric hand mixer

3 saucepans (2-liter, 1-liter, and ½-liter capacities)

3 mixing bowls of varying sizes

RECOMMENDED SPECIAL EQUIPMENT

Piping bag with multiple tips

Molds in a variety of shapes and sizes (for popsicles, tartlets, dome cakes, etc.)

Stainless steel rings

Acetate strips

Culinary torch

RECOMMENDED SPECIAL INGREDIENTS

Most of the ice cream recipes in this book call for the following ingredients. They can be sourced online, and each is critical to the overall texture of the finished product. (Inulin is another stabilizer that shows up a couple of times in the book, though not as often as these other ingredients.)

Atomized glucose

Skim milk powder

Ice cream or sorbet stabilizer

TIPS BEFORE YOU START MAKING ICE CREAM AND SORBET RECIPES

A good ice cream or sorbet depends on the proper balance between ingredients: fat, sugar, eggs, stabilizers or gelatin, dairy, and fruit. I've done the work of calibrating these formulas for you, since there's no such thing as one mother recipe for ice cream or sorbet. Here are the key principles for success:

RULE NO. 1: Precision
For best results, measure ingredients using a scale that reads in grams. For cooking, always use a probe thermometer to ensure precise temperature control.

RULE NO. 2: Ingredient quality
Choose excellent dairy; fresh, high-quality eggs; and ripe, healthy fruit. You can't make exceptional ice cream or sorbet without the best nature has to offer. Unless specified otherwise, eggs are large, butter is unsalted, and salt is kosher. In addition, purchasing untreated or organic citrus is expensive but it's well worth it when recipes call for zest. If that's not an option, wash your citrus well before using.

RULE NO. 3: Pasteurization
For custard-style ice creams, cook the mixture to at least 181 to 185°F (83 to 85°C). This step, along with rapidly cooling it in the freezer to 39°F (4°C), is crucial for food safety and for achieving the desired final texture. Cooking at this temperature gives the ice cream a creamier mouthfeel.

RULE NO. 4: Aging
For all ice cream and sorbet bases, let the mixture rest in the refrigerator for at least 4 hours. This step is essential for developing the right texture—smooth, light, and aromatic. It also allows dry ingredients, like milk powder, to fully hydrate. Sugars will bind and stabilize the water content (ice cream formulas typically contain about 40 percent dry matter and 60 percent liquid).

RULE NO. 5: Homogenization
Use an immersion blender to blend the base after cooking and again after aging. This breaks down ingredients further and ensures a finer texture.

RULE NO. 6: Post-churn freezing
Once churned, let the ice cream rest in the freezer for at least 10 minutes before working with it. This helps firm it up for easier handling.

STABILIZERS

If you can't find stabilizers, here's a workaround to achieve a similar texture for quick-consumption recipes. Replace the stabilizer with an equal weight of sheet or powdered gelatin.

FOR SHEET GELATIN

INGREDIENT

2 teaspoons (10 g) of stabilizer can be replaced with 10 g of sheet gelatin.

METHOD

Soak the gelatin sheets in seven times their weight in cold water. Let them sit in the refrigerator for at least 20 minutes, then drain. Add the hydrated and drained sheets to the mixture after cooking.

FOR POWDERED GELATIN

INGREDIENT

2 teaspoons (10 g) of stabilizer can be replaced with 2 teaspoons (10 g) of powdered gelatin.

METHOD

Whisk the gelatin powder into six times its weight in warm water. Let it set, then melt it at 86°F (30°C), whisking well. Add the melted gelatin after the mixture is cooked.

TYPES OF ICE CREAM MACHINES

HOME ICE CREAM MAKERS

Don't hesitate to invest in a quality model with enough power (around 180 W) to churn the recipes in this book properly. Avoid machines that require pre-freezing a bowl—they often lack the strength to produce good results.

Look for machines that chill the churning bowl to sub-zero temperatures. For ideal churning, the base should reach a temperature between 25°F and 21°F (-4 to -6°C).

Also pay attention to paddle speed: the faster it turns, the better the texture of your ice cream. Churning time for this type of machine is generally 20 to 30 minutes.

THERMOMIX

If you're using a Thermomix to churn the recipes, follow these instructions for sorbets:

Freeze diced fruit for at least 4 hours—this is essential. Also freeze the sorbet syrup for 4 hours minimum. To churn, place the frozen fruit and syrup in the Thermomix bowl and blend. The freezing effect combined with the machine's power and blade speed will do the work.

PACOJET

Widely used in professional kitchens, the Pacojet yields excellent results. Follow the recipe instructions in the book, then chill the finished mix to 39°F (4°C). Transfer it to the Pacojet beaker and freeze it for at least 6 hours until fully solid.

To churn, place the frozen beaker on the Pacojet and process. You can choose to portion just part of the contents or the entire batch.

PROFESSIONAL TURBINES

Simply follow the methods laid out in the recipes. The ideal churning temperature with these machines is between 21°F and 18°F (-6 to -8°C).

ICE CREAM & SORBETS

Emmanuel Ryon makes ice cream first for himself, and if others enjoy it, all the better. For him, ice cream isn't just a scoop in a bowl. It's a mindset, a creative process, an art form. He builds his flavors from scratch, experimenting and refining. He delights in surprising ingredients like black garlic, asparagus, and green peas. He's always searching for new textures and pushing boundaries.

With each recipe, his goal is to revisit the classics while adding a layer of indulgence. He wants to surprise, even disrupt, the way we experience flavor. In his asparagus and tonka bean ice cream, he challenges himself: how can you make asparagus taste indulgent? By carefully balancing flavor and texture, he brings out its roasted bitter almond notes and enhances them with a tonka bean.

Sweet pea basil ice cream? It's the kind of pairing only Emmanuel would dare imagine. What inspires him is the intense natural sweetness of the peas, combined with the cold texture of the frozen base. Add basil, and the recipe takes on complexity and becomes truly satisfying.

His ideas often come from everyday life and encounters with growers and artisans. One example: his Maragogipe coffee ice cream with caramelized coffee skin was born after meeting a roaster in France's Drôme region who was working with Maragogipe, a large, round-grained Mexican coffee. The roaster wasn't using the coffee's thick outer membrane, which has a distinct hazelnut flavor. That meeting inspired a recipe that expresses notes of both coffee and hazelnut from a single raw ingredient.

The strawberry sorbet with Tagada chips was inspired by memories from his own childhood, or really childhood in general. He wanted to create a dessert just for kids. That's when he thought of baking Tagada strawberry candies in the oven. The result was surprising. They turned crisp and chip-like, with a texture and look that reminded him of a slice of Kobe beef. The contrast really made him smile.

AVOCADO VANILLA ICE CREAM WITH CHESTNUT CREAM

Prep time: 20 minutes

Cook time: 10 minutes

Chill time: 4 hours

Freeze time: 10 minutes after churning

Serves: 8

1 vanilla bean

2 cups (480 ml) whole milk

½ cup (120 ml) heavy cream

½ cup (100 g) granulated sugar

½ cup (100 g) atomized glucose

½ cup (60 g) skim milk powder

1½ tsp (6 g) ice cream stabilizer

¾ cup (200 g) avocado (about 1 ½ avocados)

FOR SERVING

8 tbsp chestnut cream

1 Using a knife, split the vanilla bean lengthwise and scrape out the seeds.

2 In a saucepan, combine the milk, cream, vanilla seeds, and the bean pod. Bring to a boil, then add the sugar, glucose, milk powder, and stabilizer.

3 Stir gently and heat the mixture to 181°F (83°C) checking with probe thermometer. Remove the vanilla bean.

4 Scoop out the avocado flesh and add it to the warm mixture. Blend with an immersion blender until smooth, then transfer to a heatproof container. Cool quickly in the freezer to 39°F (4°C).

5 Once chilled, let the mixture rest in the refrigerator for 4 hours.

6 Blend the mixture again and churn in an ice cream maker. Freeze for 10 minutes after churning.

PLATING

7 Place the serving plates in the freezer for 10 minutes before serving.

8 Just before serving, use a spoon to draw a swoosh of chestnut cream on the chilled plates. Place a scoop of avocado vanilla ice cream on top.

CHEF'S TIP

If you like, you can mix 1 tbsp of whisky with the chestnut cream. I love this combination.

JERUSALEM ARTICHOKE ICE CREAM WITH ARTICHOKE CRISPS

Prep time: 1 hour

Cook time: 1 hour 40 minutes

Chill time: 4 hours

Freeze time: 10 minutes after churning

Serves: 8

JERUSALEM ARTICHOKE PURÉE

10 ½ oz (300 g) Jerusalem artichokes

2 cups (480 ml) whole milk

JERUSALEM ARTICHOKE ICE CREAM

2 cups (480 ml) whole milk

⅔ cup (160 ml) heavy cream

¼ tsp vanilla powder

⅛ tsp salt

½ cup + 1 tbsp (110 g) granulated sugar

½ cup + 1 tbsp (105 g) atomized glucose

½ cup (60 g) skim milk powder

1 ½ tsp ice cream stabilizer

1 cup (250 g) Jerusalem artichoke purée (recipe following)

ARTICHOKE CRISPS

Reserved Jerusalem artichoke peels

CRUNCHY GARNISH

1 cup (240 ml) milk

¼ cup (50 g) granulated sugar

½ cup (60 g) rice flour

⅛ tsp vanilla powder

JERUSALEM ARTICHOKE PURÉE

1 Wash and peel the Jerusalem artichokes, saving the peels for the crisps.

2 In a medium saucepan bring the milk and 2 cups (480 ml) of water to a boil. Simmer the peeled artichokes in the milk and water until tender. Strain the mixture through a fine mesh strainer (discarding the liquid) and blend the artichokes until smooth using an immersion blender. Set aside.

JERUSALEM ARTICHOKE ICE CREAM

3 In a saucepan, combine the milk, cream, vanilla powder, and salt. Bring to a boil, then add the sugar, glucose, milk powder, and stabilizer.

4 Stir well and heat to 181°F (83°C), checking with a probe thermometer.

5 Remove from the heat and stir in Jerusalem artichoke purée. Blend thoroughly with an immersion mixer, then transfer to a heatproof container. Cool quickly in the freezer to 39°F (4°C).

6 Once chilled, let the base rest in the refrigerator for 4 hours. Blend again and churn in an ice cream maker. Freeze for 10 minutes after churning.

CRISPS

7 Preheat the oven to 250°F (120°C). Rinse and lightly pat the peels dry. Spread them on a baking sheet and bake for 1 hour. Set aside.

CRUNCHY GARNISH

8 Preheat the oven to 175°F (80°C). In a saucepan, bring the milk to a boil. Whisk in the sugar, rice flour, and vanilla powder. Bring the mixture back to a boil, then blend with an immersion blender until smooth.

9 Spread the batter onto a nonstick baking sheet and bake for 30 minutes. Remove from the oven, cool, and store in a dry place.

PLATING

10 Scoop the Jerusalem artichoke ice cream into a bowl or onto a plate, then top with the crisp peels and the crunchy garnish for contrast.

CHEF'S TIP

I like to add a drop of Cointreau to the Jerusalem artichoke ice cream for a refreshing finish.

ASPARAGUS AND TONKA BEAN ICE CREAM

Prep time: 1 hour

Cook time: 25 minutes

Chilling time: 4 hours

Freeze time: 10 minutes after churning

Serves: 8

ASPARAGUS PURÉE

2.2 lb (1 kg) white asparagus

Salt to taste

ASPARAGUS AND TONKA BEAN ICE CREAM

2 cups (480 ml) whole milk

1 ¼ cups (300 ml) heavy cream

1 tonka bean, grated

¾ cup (150 g) granulated sugar

⅓ cup (70 g) atomized glucose

¼ tsp vanilla powder

⅛ tsp salt

½ cup (60 g) nonfat dry milk powder

1 ¼ tsp ice cream stabilizer

1 ¼ cups (300 ml) asparagus purée (recipe following)

ASPARAGUS PURÉE

1. Trim the asparagus stalks 1 ½ inches (3 ½ cm) from the base and peel them with a vegetable peeler.
2. In a saucepan, boil the asparagus in salted water for 15 to 20 minutes. Prepare a bowl of ice water.
3. Chill the drained asparagus in the ice water.
4. Blend the cooled asparagus in a small food processor and strain through a fine mesh sieve to remove fibers.

ASPARAGUS AND TONKA BEAN ICE CREAM

5. In a saucepan, combine the milk, cream, and grated tonka bean. Bring to a boil, then add the sugar, glucose, vanilla powder, salt, dry milk, and stabilizer.
6. Stir and heat the mixture to 181°F (83°C) checking with a probe thermometer.
7. Remove from the heat, add the asparagus purée, and blend thoroughly with an immersion blender. Transfer to a heatproof container and cool quickly in the freezer to 39°F (4°C).
8. Once chilled, refrigerate for 4 hours to infuse.
9. Blend again, then churn in an ice cream maker. Freeze for 10 minutes after churning.

CHEF'S TIP

This ice cream is delicious with chilled pea soup.

VANILLA CUSTARD ICE CREAM

Prep time: 30 minutes

Cook time: 10 minutes

Chilling time: 4 hours

Freeze time: 20 minutes after churning

Serves: 6

2 vanilla beans

2 cups (480 ml) whole milk

⅔ cup (160 ml) heavy cream

2 tbsp acacia honey

5 egg yolks

⅔ cup (130 g) granulated sugar, divided

½ cup (50 g) nonfat dry milk powder

½ tsp ice cream stabilizer

1. Using a knife, split the vanilla beans lengthwise and scrape out the seeds.
2. In a saucepan, combine the milk, cream, honey, and vanilla seeds and pods. Bring to a boil.
3. In a mixing bowl, whisk the egg yolks with 2 tbsp of the sugar until pale.
4. Pour the hot mixture over the yolks, whisk well, then return the custard to the saucepan. Add the remaining sugar, dry milk, and stabilizer.
5. Stir gently and heat to 181°F (83°C), checking with a thermometer.
6. Strain through a chinois strainer, remove the vanilla pods, blend with an immersion blender, and transfer to a heatproof container. Cool quickly in the freezer to 39°F (4°C).
7. Once chilled, let the custard infuse for 4 hours in the fridge.
8. Blend again and churn. Freeze for 20 minutes after churning.

CHEF'S TIP

Don't throw out used vanilla pods. Rinse them, boil them to clean, then dry them in the oven at 195°F (90°C) for 1 hour. Once dried, blend into powder and store in a jar. Use this powdered vanilla to flavor baked goods or beverages. Mix it with sugar to create vanilla sugar to use in place of granulated sugar in baking recipes.

TANZANIAN CHOCOLATE ICE CREAM

Prep time: 30 minutes

Cook time: 10 minutes

Chilling time: 4 hours

Freeze time: 10 minutes after churning

Serves: 6

2 cups (480 ml) whole milk

⅓ cup (80 ml) heavy cream

2 tbsp invert sugar

4 egg yolks

½ cup (100 g) granulated sugar, divided

¼ cup (25 g) nonfat dry milk powder

½ tsp ice cream stabilizer

5 ⅓ oz (150 g) 75 percent cacao Tanzanian dark chocolate

1. In a saucepan, combine the milk, cream, and invert sugar. Bring to a boil.
2. In a mixing bowl, whisk the yolks with 1 ½ tbsp of the sugar. Pour the hot liquid over the yolks, whisking constantly. Return the custard to the saucepan and add the rest of the sugar, dry milk, and stabilizer.
3. Stir gently and heat to 185°F (85°C), checking with a thermometer.
4. Chop the chocolate and add it to the hot mixture. Blend with an immersion blender and transfer to a heatproof container. Chill in the freezer until the temperature reaches 39°F (4°C).
5. Once chilled, infuse for 4 hours in the refrigerator.
6. Blend again and churn. Freeze for 10 minutes after churning.

CHEF'S TIP

Invert sugar is sweeter than granulated sugar, because it's a syrup, it's less likely to crystallize when frozen. While some well-stocked grocery stores might stock invert sugar, it's easiest to order it online. In a pinch, you can substitute a combination of honey and corn syrup, but the final flavor will be slightly different.

MARAGOGIPE COFFEE ICE CREAM WITH CARAMELIZED COFFEE SKIN

Prep time: 40 minutes

Cook time: 25 minutes

Infusion time: 1 hour

Chilling time: 4 hours

Freeze time: 10 minutes after churning

Serves: 6

COFFEE ICE CREAM

2 ½ oz (70 g) Maragogipe coffee beans

2 ⅓ cups (560 ml) whole milk

⅔ cup (160 ml) heavy cream

2 egg yolks

⅔ cup (130 g) granulated sugar, divided

3 tbsp atomized glucose

⅓ cup (40 g) nonfat dry milk powder

½ tsp ice cream stabilizer

CARAMELIZED COFFEE SKINS

1 tbsp coffee skins (see Chef's Tip)

1 tbsp powdered sugar

COFFEE ICE CREAM

1 Preheat the oven to 285°F (140°C). Spread the coffee beans on a baking sheet and roast for 10 minutes. Crush them with a mortar and pestle and mix the resulting powder with the milk.

2 Let infuse at room temperature for 1 hour, then strain through a chinois strainer.

3 In a saucepan, combine the milk infusion with the cream, stir, and bring to a boil.

4 In a mixing bowl, whisk the yolks with 2 tbsp of the sugar. Pour the hot liquid over the yolks, whisk, return to the saucepan, and add the remaining sugar, glucose, dry milk, and stabilizer.

5 Stir gently and heat to 185°F (85°C), checking with a thermometer. Blend with an immersion blender, and transfer to a heatproof container. Cool quickly in the freezer to 39°F (4°C).

6 Once chilled, infuse for at least 4 hours in the refrigerator.

7 Blend again and churn. Freeze for 10 minutes after churning.

CARAMELIZED COFFEE SKINS

8 Preheat the oven to 250°F (120°C). Spread the coffee skins on a baking sheet lined with parchment paper. Dust with powdered sugar and bake for 12 minutes. Set aside.

PLATING

9 Chill small bowls in the freezer. Just before serving, place a scoop of Maragogipe coffee ice cream in each bowl and sprinkle with caramelized coffee skins.

CHEF'S TIP

Ask your roaster to save the coffee skins that come off the beans during roasting. Their flavor blends notes of hazelnut, coffee, and honey and is absolutely worth discovering.

COINTREAU SWIRL ICE CREAM WITH LEMON CREAM

Prep time: 1 hour

Cook time: 2 hours 30 minutes

Chill time: 4 hours

Infusion time: 4 hours

Freeze time: 1 hour

Serves: 8

COINTREAU ICE CREAM

2 cups (480 ml) whole milk

¾ cup (180 ml) heavy cream

1 tsp lemon zest

2 egg yolks

½ cup + 1 tbsp (110 g) granulated sugar

3 tbsp atomized glucose

1 tsp (5 g) ice cream stabilizer

½ cup (50 g) nonfat milk powder

2 tbsp Cointreau

LEMON CREAM

¾ cup + 1 tbsp (210 g) lemon juice

¼ cup (60 g) butter

1 tsp lemon zest

3 eggs

¾ cup + 1 tbsp (170 g) granulated sugar

SOFT MERINGUE

5 egg whites

1 cup (200 g) granulated sugar, divided

½ cup (55 g) powdered sugar, sifted

ITALIAN MERINGUE WITH IRANIAN BLACK LEMON

¾ cup (150 g) granulated sugar

1 tbsp atomized glucose

2 egg whites

⅛ tsp Iranian black lemon powder

COINTREAU ICE CREAM

1 In a saucepan, bring the milk, cream, and zest to a boil.

2 In a mixing bowl, whisk the egg yolks with the sugar, atomized glucose, stabilizer, and milk powder until pale.

3 Off the heat, gradually pour the hot mixture over the egg yolk mixture, whisking constantly. Return to the saucepan and cook until it reaches 185°F (85°C), checking with a probe thermometer.

4 Strain through a fine mesh sieve and blend with an immersion blender. Transfer to a heatproof container and chill rapidly in the freezer to 39°F (4°C).

5 Once chilled, refrigerate for 4 hours. Stir in the Cointreau and allow it to infuse for at least 4 more hours.

6 Blend again and churn in the ice cream machine.

LEMON CREAM

7 In a saucepan, heat the lemon juice, butter, and zest until boiling.

8 In a bowl, whisk the eggs with the sugar until pale.

9 Gradually pour the hot liquid over the eggs, whisking, then return to the saucepan and heat to 181°F (83°C).

10 Using an immersion blender, blend until smooth. Transfer to a heatproof bowl and chill in the freezer to 39°F (4°C), then refrigerate for at least four hours.

SOFT MERINGUE

11 Preheat the oven to 175°F (80°C).

12 In a bowl, beat the egg whites with 1 ½ tbsp of the granulated sugar using an electric mixer.

13 Gradually add ⅓ cup (80 g) of the granulated sugar while continuing to whip. When the meringue begins to firm up, fold in the remaining granulated sugar. Finally, gently fold in the sifted powdered sugar using a spatula.

14 Pipe the meringue onto a baking sheet lined with parchment paper. Bake for 2 hours.

ITALIAN MERINGUE WITH IRANIAN BLACK LEMON

15 In a saucepan, combine ¼ cup (60 g) water, sugar, and glucose and heat to 244°F (118°C).

16 Meanwhile, beat the egg whites with an electric mixer until frothy. Slowly pour the hot syrup over the whites, add the black lemon powder, and continue beating until the meringue has cooled completely.

COINTREAU ICE CREAM WITH LEMON CREAM SWIRL

17 Place an ice cream container in the freezer.

18 Whisk the chilled lemon cream. In the cold container, spread a layer of Cointreau ice cream, then a layer of lemon cream, reserving some for garnish. Freeze for 20 minutes. Add another layer of Cointreau ice cream.

PLATING

19 Fill a piping bag, fitted with a plain No. 8 tip, with the Italian meringue. On a plate, pipe a 4-inch (10-cm) meringue strip and lightly torch the surface.

20 Add a few dots of lemon cream to the plate, then place a scoop of the Cointreau and lemon cream ice cream. Garnish with crumbled soft meringue.

NYONS OLIVE OIL ICE CREAM

Prep time: 20 minutes

Cook time: 10 minutes

Chill time: 4 hours

Freeze time: 10 minutes after churning

Serves: 6

2 cups (480 ml) whole milk

⅓ cup + 1 tbsp (100 g) heavy cream

2 tsp fresh thyme

¼ tsp salt

½ cup (100 g) granulated sugar

¼ cup (50 g) atomized glucose

½ cup (50 g) nonfat milk powder

1 tsp ice cream stabilizer

⅓ cup + 1 tbsp (95 ml) Nyons black olive oil macerate, plus more for serving

1. In a saucepan, combine the milk, cream, thyme, and salt. Bring to a boil.
2. Stir in the sugar, atomized glucose, milk powder, and stabilizer.
3. Mix and heat to 181°F (83°C), checking with a probe thermometer.
4. Strain and blend with an immersion blender. Transfer to a heatproof container and cool quickly in the freezer to 39°F (4°C).
5. Stir in the olive oil gently and refrigerate for 4 hours.
6. Blend again and churn. Freeze for 10 minutes after churning.

PLATING

7. Scoop out balls of ice cream.
8. Use the back of a spoon to form a well in the center of each one. Freeze again.
9. Just before serving, pour a drizzle of Nyons olive oil macerate into the well.

CHEF'S TIP

If you can find Nyons olive oil macerate online, you'll appreciate the earthy flavors that the oil imparts. If you can't, substitute another excellent quality olive oil.

SWEET PEA BASIL ICE CREAM

Prep time: 40 minutes

Cook time: 20 minutes

Chill time: 4 hours

Freeze time: 10 minutes after churning

Serves: 8

SWEET PEA PURÉE

2 cups (400 g) fresh peas

SWEET PEA BASIL ICE CREAM

2 cups (480 ml) whole milk

¾ cup (180 ml) heavy cream

1 tbsp fresh basil

½ tsp salt

½ cup (100 g) granulated sugar

⅓ cup (80 g) inulin

½ cup + 1 tbsp (105 g) atomized glucose

½ cup + 1 tbsp (60 g) nonfat milk powder

1 ¼ tsp ice cream stabilizer

1 cup (250 g) sweet pea purée (recipe following)

FOR SERVING

Cooked peas

Fresh basil leaves

Olive oil

SWEET PEA PURÉE

1 Bring 4 ¼ cups (1 liter) of water to a boil in a saucepan. Add the peas and cook until tender.

2 Drain and, using an immersion blender, blend until smooth. Strain through a fine sieve and set aside.

SWEET PEA BASIL ICE CREAM

3 In a saucepan, combine the milk, cream, basil, and salt. Bring to a boil.

4 Add the sugar, inulin, glucose, milk powder, and stabilizer.

5 Mix and heat to 185°F (85°C), checking with a probe thermometer. Blend thoroughly with an immersion blender.

6 Pour over the strained pea purée and blend again. Transfer to a heatproof container and chill to 39°F (4°C).

7 Refrigerate for 4 hours.

8 Blend again and churn. Freeze for 10 minutes after churning.

PLATING

9 Chill serving plates in the freezer. Fill a piping bag, fitted with a plain No. 3 pastry tip, with the ice cream.

10 At serving time, pipe three large dots of ice cream onto the chilled plate, then use a spatula to drag them into swooshes. Garnish with cooked peas, basil leaves, and drops of olive oil using a pipette.

BUCKWHEAT HONEY CARAMEL ICE CREAM

Prep time: 40 minutes

Cook time: 20 minutes

Chill time: 4 hours

Freeze time: 10 minutes after churning

Serves: 6

CARAMEL HONEY ICE CREAM

½ cup (100 g) granulated sugar

1 ½ tbsp salted butter

1 ½ tbsp buckwheat honey

1 cup (240 ml) heavy cream

2 cups (480 ml) whole milk

⅓ cup (80 g) atomized glucose

⅓ cup (50 g) skim milk powder

¾ tsp ice cream stabilizer

¼ tsp fleur de sel

BUCKWHEAT CARAMEL SAUCE

1 tbsp buckwheat honey

½ cup + 2 tbsp (125 g) granulated sugar

½ cup (120 ml) heavy cream

CARAMEL HONEY ICE CREAM

1. In a saucepan over medium heat, make a dry caramel by allowing the sugar to caramelize and turn golden brown. Swirl the saucepan if necessary for even browning, but do not stir.
2. Once caramel is golden brown, add the butter and stir well. Stir in the honey, cream, and milk, then bring to a boil.
3. Remove from the heat. Add the atomized glucose, milk powder, stabilizer, and fleur de sel. Stir to combine.
4. Return to the stove and cook until the temperature reaches 185°F (85°C), checking with a probe thermometer. Using an immersion blender, blend thoroughly, then transfer to a heatproof container. Cool quickly in the freezer to 39°F (4°C).
5. Once cooled, let the mixture infuse in the fridge for 4 hours.
6. Blend again and churn in your ice cream maker. Freeze for 10 minutes after churning.

BUCKWHEAT CARAMEL SAUCE

7. In a saucepan, cook the honey and sugar until caramelized.
8. In a separate saucepan, gently heat the cream, then add it to the caramel. Simmer for 1 minute.
9. Whisk to combine and let cool at room temperature.
10. Swirl the cooled caramel into the ice cream after churning.

PLATING

11. Scoop and serve in a bowl, a Classic Cone (page 224), or a Chocolate Cone (page 224).

CHEF'S TIP

To help prevent overflow when adding cream or butter to the hot sugar, use a larger saucepan for the caramel.

VANILLA POPCORN ICE CREAM

Prep time: 40 minutes

Cook time: 20 minutes

Chill time: 4 hours

Freeze time: 20 minutes after churning

Serves: 6

VANILLA ICE CREAM

2 vanilla beans

2 cups (480 ml) whole milk

⅔ cup (160 ml) heavy cream

2 egg yolks

⅔ cup (140 g) granulated sugar, divided

3 tbsp atomized glucose

⅓ cup (40 g) skim milk powder

¾ tsp ice cream stabilizer

POPCORN

1 tsp neutral oil

1 tbsp popcorn kernels

CARAMEL SAUCE

½ cup + 2 tbsp (110 g) granulated sugar

2 tbsp glucose

1 ¼ cups (300 ml) heavy cream

3 tbsp butter

VANILLA ICE CREAM

1. Split the vanilla beans and scrape out the seeds.
2. Combine the milk, cream, vanilla seeds, and pods in a saucepan. Bring to a boil.
3. In a bowl, whisk the egg yolks with 2 tbsp of the sugar until pale. Pour in the hot milk mixture and whisk to combine. Return the mixture to the saucepan and stir in the remaining sugar, atomized glucose, milk powder, and stabilizer.
4. Cook gently to 185°F (85°C), then strain through a fine mesh sieve and remove the pods. Blend with an immersion blender and transfer to a heatproof container. Cool rapidly in the freezer to 39°F (4°C).
5. Once cooled, refrigerate for 4 hours to infuse.
6. Blend again and churn in your ice cream maker. Freeze for 20 minutes after churning.

POPCORN

7. Pour the oil into a large pot with a lid and heat over high heat for a few minutes. Add the popcorn kernels, reduce the heat to medium and cover the pot with the lid. Shake to distribute the hot oil a few times during popping. Once the popping slows down, remove from the heat but keep the lid on until the popping stops completely.

CARAMEL SAUCE

8. In a copper or heavy-bottomed saucepan, cook the sugar and glucose to 392°F (200°C).
9. In another saucepan, gently warm the cream. When the caramel is ready, pour in the warm cream and stir.
10. Off the heat, stir in the butter and mix well. Reserve for serving.

PLATING

11. Chill a large plate lined with plastic wrap in the freezer.
12. Scoop balls of vanilla ice cream onto the plastic-lined plate and press popcorn into one side of each scoop.
13. On serving plates, drizzle caramel sauce with a spoon. Lift each ice cream popcorn ball from the plastic-lined plate and arrange them on plates with the caramel drizzle.

CHEF'S TIP

To prevent the caramel from bubbling over, you can pre-whip the heavy cream with an electric mixer before adding it.

MALAGA ICE CREAM

Prep time: 30 minutes

Cook time: 10 minutes

Chill time: 4 hours

Freeze time: 10 minutes after churning

Serves: 8

RUM-SOAKED RAISINS

1 cup (150 g) Malaga raisins

3 tbsp Mount Gay dark rum

MALAGA ICE CREAM

2 cups (480 ml) whole milk

¾ cup (180 ml) heavy cream

¾ cup (150 g) granulated sugar, divided

3 tbsp atomized glucose

⅓ cup (50 g) skim milk powder

1 tsp ice cream stabilizer

2 egg yolks

¼ cup (60 ml) Mount Gay dark rum

1 cup (150 g) rum-soaked raisins (recipe following)

RUM-SOAKED RAISINS

1 Rinse the raisins.

2 In a saucepan, bring ⅓ cup (80 ml) of water and the raisins to a boil. Simmer until the water has evaporated and the raisins are plump.

3 Add the rum and flambé. Set aside.

MALAGA ICE CREAM

4 In a saucepan, bring the milk and cream to a boil. Add ⅔ cup (125 g) of the sugar, the atomized glucose, milk powder, and stabilizer.

5 In a bowl, whisk the yolks with the remaining sugar.

6 Pour the hot milk mixture over the yolks, whisking well. Return the mixture to the saucepan and heat to 185°F (85°C).

7 Blend the custard with an immersion blender and transfer to a heatproof container. Cool quickly in the freezer to 39°F (4°C).

8 Once chilled, stir in the rum and refrigerate for 4 hours.

9 Blend again and churn in your ice cream maker.

10 After churning, fold the rum-soaked raisins into the ice cream. Freeze for 10 minutes.

CHEF'S TIP

For a twist, add 2 tsp of Marsala wine to enhance the final flavor.

BLACK GARLIC ICE CREAM

Prep time: 15 minutes

Cook time: 10 minutes

Chill time: 4 hours

Freeze time: 10 minutes after churning

Serves: 6

2 cups (480 ml) whole milk

¾ cup (180 ml) heavy cream

1 tbsp black garlic purée

½ cup (100 g) granulated sugar

⅓ cup (80 g) atomized glucose

½ cup (50 g) skim milk powder

1 ½ tsp ice cream stabilizer

1 In a saucepan, combine the milk, cream, and black garlic. Stir and bring to a boil. Add the sugar, atomized glucose, skim milk powder, and stabilizer.

2 Stir and heat the mixture to 185°F (85°C), checking with a probe thermometer.

3 Blend thoroughly with an immersion blender, then transfer to a heatproof bowl. Chill quickly in the freezer to 39°F (4°C).

4 Once chilled, let the mixture steep in the refrigerator for 4 hours.

5 Blend again, then churn in an ice cream maker. Freeze for 10 minutes after churning.

PLATING

6 Plate a scoop alongside a summer salad or a winter soup.

CHEF'S TIP

This is one of the most original ice creams in my collection. Its flavor is extraordinary—somewhere between licorice, brown sugar, and balsamic vinegar, it's a rare complexity that I love. Black garlic has long been used in Korean and Japanese cuisine. I use garlic from the Boutarin family in the Drôme region of France. They process it with traditional Japanese methods, and it's a true gem.

PLOMBIÈRES ICE CREAM

Prep time: 30 minutes

Maceration time: 8 hours

Cook time: 10 minutes

Chill time: 4 hours

Freeze time: 10 minutes after churning

Serves: 8

MACERATED CANDIED FRUIT MIX

2 tbsp candied citron

2 tbsp candied cherries

2 tbsp candied orange peel

2 tbsp candied lemon peel

2 tbsp candied angelica

3 tbsp Fougerolles kirsch

ICE CREAM BASE

2 cups (480 ml) whole milk

¾ cup (180 ml) heavy cream

3 tbsp 50 percent almond paste

⅓ cup (70 g) granulated sugar

⅓ cup (70 g) atomized glucose

½ cup (50 g) skim milk powder

1 tsp ice cream stabilizer

⅔ cup (165 g) macerated candied fruit mix (recipe following)

CANDIED FRUIT MIX

1. Dice the candied fruit into ¾-inch (2-cm) cubes.
2. Place the fruit in a bowl with the kirsch and let soak for 8 hours.

PLOMBIÈRES ICE CREAM

3. In a saucepan, combine the milk, cream, and almond paste. Stir and bring to a boil. Add the sugar, atomized glucose, skim milk powder, and stabilizer.
4. Stir and heat to 185°F (85°C), checking with a probe thermometer.
5. Blend the mixture with an immersion blender and transfer to a heatproof container. Cool quickly in the freezer to 39°F (4°C).
6. Once chilled, refrigerate for 4 hours to infuse.
7. Blend again, then churn in an ice cream maker.
8. Fold in the macerated candied fruit mix after churning. Freeze for 10 minutes.

CHEF'S TIP

Be sure to use Fougerolles kirsch—the spirit gives the ice cream its signature flavor and indulgence.

Candied citron and angelica can be sourced online.

ROSE PETAL SORBET

Prep time: 20 minutes

Infusion time: 24 hours

Cook time: 10 minutes

Chill time: 4 hours

Freeze time: 20 minutes after churning

Serves: 6

2 tbsp rose petals

½ cup (90 g) granulated sugar

½ cup (115 g) atomized glucose

1 tsp sorbet stabilizer

1. In a container, heat 2 cups (480 ml) of water to 86°F (30°C). Add the rose petals and infuse for 24 hours. Strain through a fine mesh sieve.
2. Pour the rose infusion into a saucepan and bring to a boil.
3. Add the sugar, atomized glucose, and stabilizer.
4. Stir and heat to 181°F (83°C), checking with a probe thermometer.
5. Blend well with an immersion blender and transfer to a heatproof container. Cool quickly in the freezer to 39°F (4°C).
6. Refrigerate for at least 4 hours.
7. Blend again and churn. Freeze for 20 minutes after churning.

CHEF'S TIP

To fully extract the rose's fragrance, it's crucial to steep the petals in 86°F (30°C) water.

APRICOT VERBENA SORBET

Prep time: 20 minutes

Cook time: 10 minutes

Chill time: 4 hours

Freeze time: 20 minutes after churning

Serves: 6

1 tbsp fresh lemon verbena leaves

⅔ cup (140 g) granulated sugar

scant ⅓ cup (50 g) atomized glucose

1 tsp sorbet stabilizer

1 ¾ cups (420 ml) apricot purée

2 tsp lemon juice

FOR SERVING

Fresh lemon verbena leaves

1 In a saucepan, bring ½ cup (120 ml) of water to a boil with the verbena leaves.
2 Add the sugar, atomized glucose, and stabilizer.
3 Stir and heat to 212°F (100°C), checking with a probe thermometer.
4 Blend with an immersion blender and strain through a fine mesh sieve.
5 Add the apricot purée and lemon juice, and blend again.
6 Transfer to a heatproof bowl and cool quickly in the freezer to 39°F (4°C), then refrigerate for 4 hours.
7 Blend once more and churn. Freeze for 20 minutes after churning.

PLATING

8 Place six mini scoops of apricot verbena sorbet in a small dish and garnish with fresh verbena leaves.

CHEF'S TIP

If possible, use ripe Bergeron apricots for the purée. They deliver the richest flavor.

CORSICAN CLEMENTINE SORBET

Prep time: 20 minutes

Cook time: 10 minutes

Chill time: 24 hours

Freeze time: 10 minutes after churning

Serves: 6

6 Corsican clementines

2 sugar cubes

2 cups (480 ml) Corsican clementine juice, divided

generous 1 cup (120 g) granulated sugar

⅓ cup (80 g) atomized glucose

¾ tsp sorbet stabilizer

1 tsp lemon juice

1 Wash and dry the clementines. Rub their skins with the sugar cubes to extract the oils.

2 In a saucepan, bring ¼ cup (60 ml) of water, ⅓ cup + 1 ½ tbsp (100 ml) of clementine juice, and the sugar cubes to a boil.

3 Add the granulated sugar, atomized glucose, and stabilizer. Stir and heat to 212°F (100°C), checking with a probe thermometer.

4 Blend the mixture with an immersion blender. Add the remaining clementine juice and lemon juice, and stir. Transfer to a heatproof container and chill quickly in the freezer to 39°F (4°C).

5 Let the mixture infuse in the fridge for 24 hours.

6 Blend again and churn. Freeze for 10 minutes after churning.

STRAWBERRY SORBET WITH TAGADA CHIPS

Prep time: 30 minutes

Cook time: 20 minutes

Chill time: 4 hours

Freeze time: 10 minutes after churning

Serves: 8

STRAWBERRY SORBET

1 cup (200 g) granulated sugar

½ cup (100 g) atomized glucose

1 tsp sorbet stabilizer

2 ½ cups (600 ml) strawberry purée

2 tsp lemon juice

TAGADA CHIPS

Several Tagada strawberry candies

STRAWBERRY SORBET

1 In a saucepan, bring ⅔ cup (160 ml) of water to a boil. Add the granulated sugar, atomized glucose, and stabilizer. Stir and bring the mixture to 212°F (100°C), checking with a probe thermometer.
2 Add the strawberry purée and lemon juice, then blend with an immersion blender. Transfer to a heatproof container and chill quickly in the freezer to 39°F (4°C).
3 Let the mixture rest and infuse in the refrigerator for 4 hours.
4 Blend again and churn in an ice cream maker. Freeze for 10 minutes after churning.

TAGADA CHIPS

5 Preheat the oven to 250°F (120°C) using the convection setting. Place the Tagada candies on a baking sheet lined with parchment paper. Cover with a second sheet of parchment paper and bake for 10 minutes.
6 Remove from the oven and flatten the candies with a rolling pin.
7 Return to the oven for a few more minutes to allow the chips to fully dry. Remove, cool, and store in a dry place.

PLATING

8 Place a scoop of strawberry sorbet on each plate and decorate with the Tagada chips inserted into each scoop.

CHEF'S TIP

Tagada Candies are French gummy strawberries that—to me—taste like childhood.

FROMAGE BLANC AND GOJI BERRY SORBET

Prep time: 20 minutes

Cook time: 10 minutes

Chill time: 4 hours

Freeze time: 10 minutes

Serves: 8

¾ cup (145 g) granulated sugar

⅓ cup (80 g) atomized glucose

1 tsp sorbet stabilizer

1 cup (250 g) fromage blanc

FOR SERVING

Dried goji berries

Dried cranberries

1 In a saucepan, bring 1 ⅓ cups (320 ml) of water to a boil. Add the sugar, atomized glucose, and stabilizer.

2 Stir and heat to 181°F (83°C), checking with a probe thermometer.

3 Using an immersion blender, blend the mixture and transfer to a heatproof bowl. Cool quickly in the freezer to 39°F (4°C). Then add the fromage blanc.

4 Blend again and let infuse for at least 4 hours in the refrigerator.

5 Blend once more and churn in an ice cream maker. Freeze for 10 minutes after churning.

PLATING

6 Spoon the sorbet into dessert bowls and sprinkle with goji berries and/or dried cranberries.

CHEF'S TIP

Make sure the syrup is completely cool before adding the fromage blanc. If it's still warm, the acidity will cause it to curdle and ruin the texture of the sorbet.

TRAVEL CAKES

Travel cakes are Emmanuel's way of revisiting childhood treats and snack time for both children and adults. What really fascinates him is the portability of these cakes. Their creation implies a specific shape and a resilient texture that holds up when paired with a scoop of ice cream.

The Genoa Cake with Almond and Dragée Ice Cream is a cake baked with almond flour in a mold. Since almond has a mild flavor without acidity or bitterness, Emmanuel intensifies it by pairing the cake with almond ice cream. The result is pure almond pleasure for fans who enjoy deep, mellow flavors similar to chestnut.

In his Citrus Weekend Cake with Grapefruit Sorbet, he offers a frozen dessert that's easy to make and transport—by foot, bike, or tucked into your travel bag. The grapefruit adds boldness, fragrance, and a hint of bitterness.

And the smooth, creamy combo of the Brownie with Maple Syrup and White Chocolate Ice Cream continues the delicious journey.

MARBLE CHOCOLATE AND GREEN TEA CAKE WITH GREEN TEA ICE CREAM

Prep time: 1 hour

Cook time: 1 hour

Chill time: 4 hours

Freeze time: 10 minutes after churning

Serves: 8

GREEN TEA ICE CREAM

2 cups (480 ml) whole milk

⅔ cup (160 ml) heavy cream

½ cup + 1 tbsp (120 g) granulated sugar

⅓ cup (50 g) atomized glucose

½ cup (50 g) skim milk powder

1 tsp ice cream stabilizer

2 tbsp organic matcha green tea powder

MARBLE CAKE

1 cup + 2 tbsp (250 g) softened butter, plus more for greasing the pan

1 ½ tsp salt

1 cup (190 g) granulated sugar, divided

2 tsp vanilla extract

5 egg yolks

¼ cup (60 g) light brown sugar

5 egg whites

2 cups (250 g) all-purpose flour

½ tsp baking powder

2 tbsp cocoa powder mixed with 2 egg whites

2 tbsp matcha powder mixed with 2 egg whites

GREEN TEA ICE CREAM

1 In a saucepan, bring the milk and cream to a boil. Add the granulated sugar, atomized glucose, milk powder, and stabilizer. Mix well and heat to 181°F (83°C), checking with a probe thermometer. Add the matcha powder and stir again.

2 Blend with an immersion blender and transfer to a heatproof container. Chill quickly in the freezer to 39°F (4°C).

3 Let the mixture infuse in the refrigerator for 4 hours. Blend again and churn in an ice cream maker. Freeze for 10 minutes after churning.

MARBLE CAKE

4 In a mixing bowl, combine the softened butter with salt, ¾ cup (150 g) granulated sugar, and vanilla extract. Beat with an electric mixer and set aside.

5 In another bowl, whisk the egg yolks with the brown sugar until pale and light.

6 In yet another bowl, beat the egg whites with the remaining ¼ cup (40 g) granulated sugar with an electric mixer until stiff peaks form.

7 Combine the butter mixture with the brown sugar mixture until well combined, then gently fold in one-third of the whipped egg whites. Sift together the flour and baking powder and fold them into the batter gently with a spatula. Fold in the remaining whipped egg whites until the batter is smooth.

8 Divide the batter in half so the dough is in two separate bowls. Fold the cocoa-egg white mixture into one half. Then fold the matcha-egg white mixture into the remaining half.

9 Preheat the oven to 320°F (160°C) using the convection setting. Grease a square 6 ¼-in (16-cm), 1¾-in (4.5-cm) tall mold using a pastry brush and softened butter. Transfer each batter to a piping bag fitted with a plain No. 12 tip.

10 Pipe alternating logs of chocolate and matcha batter in three layers until both are used up. Firmly tap the cake mold on the counter to enhance the marbled effect.

11 Bake for 45 minutes. Unmold the cake while still warm.

PLATING

12 Cut the cake into rectangles about ¾ inch (2 cm) wide and 1 ½ inches (4 cm) tall. Place one rectangle on each serving plate with a scoop of green tea ice cream.

CHEF'S TIP

To check if the cake is baked through, insert a knife blade into the center—if it comes out clean, it's done.

BROWNIE WITH MAPLE SYRUP AND WHITE CHOCOLATE ICE CREAM

Prep time: 45 minutes

Baking time: 1 hour

Chilling time: 24 hours

Freeze time: 10 minutes after churning

Serves: 10

WHITE CHOCOLATE ICE CREAM

2 cups (480 ml) whole milk

½ cup (120 ml) heavy cream

2 tsp maple syrup

1 egg yolk

½ cup (90 g) granulated sugar

¼ cup (30 g) nonfat milk powder

1 tsp ice cream stabilizer

5 ⅓ oz (150 g) Zéphyr white chocolate, such as Cacao Barry

BROWNIE

1 cup (110 g) pecans

8 ¾ oz (250 g) 75 percent cacao Tanzanian chocolate

1 cup (250 g) butter, plus more for greasing

¾ cup (100 g) all-purpose flour

½ tsp (2 g) baking powder

3 eggs

1 cup (200 g) muscovado sugar

¼ tsp salt

1 ½ tsp vanilla extract

FOR SERVING

Maple syrup

WHITE CHOCOLATE ICE CREAM

1 In a saucepan, bring the milk, cream, and maple syrup to a boil.

2 In a mixing bowl, whisk the egg yolk with the sugar, milk powder, and stabilizer until pale. Pour the hot milk mixture over the yolk mixture, whisk to combine, then return the mixture to the pan. Gently heat to 181°F (83°C), checking with a probe thermometer.

3 Stir in the white chocolate, mix well, then blend using an immersion blender. Transfer to a heatproof container and cool quickly in the freezer to 39°F (4°C).

4 Let infuse in the fridge for 24 hours.

5 Blend again, then churn. Freeze for 10 minutes after churning.

BROWNIE

6 Preheat the oven to 285°F (140°C) using the convection setting. Butter a square 6 ¼-in (16-cm), 1¾-in (4.5-cm) tall mold.

7 Toast the pecans on a baking sheet for 15 minutes.

8 Melt the chocolate and butter in a double boiler at 104°F (40°C). Then set aside to cool.

9 In a small bowl, sift the flour with the baking powder.

10 In a large bowl, whisk the eggs with the muscovado sugar, salt, and vanilla until pale. Add the melted chocolate, then the sifted flour mixture. Mix well.

11 Chop the toasted pecans and add about three-quarters of the pecans to the brownie batter, reserving a few for garnish. Raise the oven temperature to 320°F (160°C).

12 Pour the batter into the prepared mold and bake for 42 minutes. Let cool and unmold.

PLATING

13 Cut strips of brownie ¾ in (2 cm) wide and 6 ¼ in (16 cm) long. Place a strip on each plate and top with a scoop of white chocolate ice cream.

14 Drizzle with maple syrup and garnish with the toasted pecans.

CHEF'S TIP

Watch the baking time closely. If the brownie is overbaked, it will become dry and crumbly.

GENOA CAKE WITH ALMOND AND DRAGÉE ICE CREAM

Prep time: 1 hour

Baking time: 30 minutes

Chilling time: 4 hours

Freeze time: 10 minutes after churning

Serves: 4

ALMOND ICE CREAM

2 cups (480 ml) whole milk

¾ cup (180 ml) heavy cream

3 ½ tbsp 50 percent almond paste

½ cup (105 g) granulated sugar

¼ cup (55 g) atomized glucose

½ cup (50 g) milk powder

1 tsp ice cream stabilizer

GENOA CAKE

6 tbsp butter, plus more for greasing

8 oz (225 g) 50 percent almond paste

½ tsp vanilla powder

3 eggs

¼ cup (30 g) all-purpose flour

¼ cup (30 g) potato starch

¼ tsp salt

2 tbsp Cointreau

½ cup (45 g) sliced almonds

FOR SERVING

Crushed dragées

ALMOND ICE CREAM

1. In a saucepan, bring the milk, cream, and almond paste to a boil. Add the sugar, glucose, milk powder, and stabilizer. Stir well and heat to 185°F (85°C), checking with a probe thermometer.
2. Blend using an immersion blender, then transfer to a heatproof container and cool quickly in the freezer to 39°F (4°C).
3. Let infuse in the fridge for 4 hours. Blend again and churn. Freeze for 10 minutes after churning.

GENOA CAKE

4. Preheat the oven to 320°F (160°C) using the convection setting. Butter a square 6 ¼-in (16-cm) sponge cake mold. Melt the butter and set aside.
5. In a stand mixer with the paddle attachment, mix the almond paste and vanilla. Add the eggs gradually and continue beating for 10 minutes.
6. Sift together the flour, potato starch, and salt. Add to the egg mixture, then fold in the Cointreau and melted butter gently with a spatula until smooth.
7. Line the prepared mold with the sliced almonds, then pour in the batter. Sprinkle more sliced almonds on top.
8. Bake for 22 minutes. Unmold while still warm.

PLATING

9. Cut the Genoa cake into rectangles 1 ½ in (4 cm) wide and 6 ¼ in (16 cm) long. Place a piece on its side on each plate to show off the almond crust.
10. Top with 1 tbsp of almond ice cream and sprinkle with crushed dragées.

CHEF'S TIP

Use hot browned butter for the Genoa cake batter to make it even softer.

Dragées are candy-coated almonds; they are also known as Jordan almonds.

CITRUS WEEKEND CAKE WITH GRAPEFRUIT SORBET

Prep time: 1 hour
Baking time: 35 minutes
Chilling time: 4 hours
Freeze time: 10 minutes after churning
Serves: 5

GRAPEFRUIT SORBET

1 ¼ cups (250 g) granulated sugar

½ cup (100 g) atomized glucose

1 tsp sorbet stabilizer

2 cups (480 ml) pink grapefruit juice

WEEKEND CAKE

6 tbsp (90 g) butter, melted, plus more for greasing

4 eggs

1 ⅓ cups (280 g) granulated sugar

1 tbsp orange blossom honey

¼ tsp salt

1 tsp orange zest

¾ cup (175 g) crème fraîche

1 cup (143 g) all-purpose flour

1 tsp baking powder

FOR SERVING

Candied orange zest

GRAPEFRUIT SORBET

1 In a saucepan, bring 1 cup (240 ml) of water to a boil, then add the sugar, glucose, and stabilizer. Stir well and heat to 185°F (85°C), checking with a probe thermometer.
2 Transfer to a heatproof container and cool quickly in the freezer to 39°F (4°C), then stir in the grapefruit juice and, using an immersion blender, blend well.
3 Let infuse in the fridge for 4 hours.
4 Strain through a fine mesh sieve, blend again, and churn. Freeze for 10 minutes after churning.

WEEKEND CAKE

5 Preheat the oven to 320°F (160°C) using the convection setting. Grease an 8-inch (20-cm) square cake mold with butter.
6 In a bowl, whisk the eggs with the sugar and honey. Add the salt and orange zest, then the crème fraîche. Mix well. Sift the flour with the baking powder. Fold into the mixture along with the melted butter.
7 Pour the batter into the prepared cake mold and bake for 30 minutes. Let cool and unmold.

PLATING

8 Cut the cake into strips 1 ½ in (4 cm) wide and 4 in (10 cm) long. On each plate, stack two strips and top with grapefruit sorbet using a spatula. Garnish with candied orange zest.

HAZELNUT FINANCIER WITH RASPBERRY AND RED BELL PEPPER SORBET

Prep time: 40 minutes

Bake time: 30 minutes

Chill time: 24 hours

Freeze time: 20 minutes after churning

Serves: 8

RASPBERRY AND RED BELL PEPPER SORBET

2 red bell peppers

1 ½ cups (350 g) raspberries

½ tsp green cardamom

¾ cup (150 g) granulated sugar, plus extra for dusting

¼ cup (65 g) atomized glucose

1 tsp sorbet stabilizer

HAZELNUT FINANCIER

5 tbsp (75 g) butter, plus extra for greasing

1 cup (100 g) hazelnut flour

1 cup (115 g) all-purpose flour

½ tsp baking powder

2 ¼ cups (280 g) powdered sugar

¼ tsp salt

1 tbsp lavender honey

8 egg whites

5 tbsp heavy cream

24 fresh raspberries

FOR SERVING

Powdered sugar

RASPBERRY AND RED BELL PEPPER SORBET

1 In a small food processor, blend the bell peppers. Strain, reserving ⅔ cup (160 ml) of juice and removing the solids. Then blend the raspberries and strain out the seeds. Combine both liquids, and set aside. Crush the green cardamom with a pestle.

2 In a saucepan, bring 1 cup (240 ml) of water to a boil with the crushed cardamom. Add the granulated sugar, atomized glucose, and sorbet stabilizer, and heat the mixture to 212°F (100°C) checking with a probe thermometer.

3 Strain through a fine mesh sieve into a heatproof container. Chill in the freezer and cool rapidly to 39°F (4°C). Stir in the raspberry purée and bell pepper juice. Mix well, then refrigerate.

4 Let infuse in the refrigerator for 24 hours. Then churn in an ice cream maker. Freeze for 20 minutes after churning.

HAZELNUT FINANCIER

5 Preheat the oven to 340°F (170°C) using the convection setting. Grease eight 4-inch (10-cm) tartlet molds with softened butter and sprinkle with granulated sugar. Tap out the excess and refrigerate the molds for 10 minutes.

6 In a mixing bowl, sift together the hazelnut flour, all-purpose flour, baking powder, and powdered sugar, then add the salt and honey. Add the egg whites and heavy cream. Mix well.

7 Make brown butter: melt the butter in a saucepan until golden brown, being careful not to burn it. Add the hot butter to the mixture and stir.

8 Pour 3 ¾ oz (110 g) of batter into each mold and add 3 raspberries per mold.

9 Bake for 20 minutes. Let cool and unmold.

PLATING

10 Using a fine sieve, dust powdered sugar around the edges of the cooled financiers.

11 Top each one with a *quenelle* of the sorbet.

FROZEN FRUIT

Emmanuel dreamed of bringing frozen fruits back into dessert fashion. They're a nostalgic nod to his childhood, when his mother and grandmother would make these refreshing treats. Simple and approachable, frozen fruits have a retro charm that brings a festive feel to family meals.

Take the Frozen Mini Halloween Squash recipe, which, by echoing the symbolism and shape of the gourd, is a playful return to childhood. First, the flesh is scooped out—just like during Halloween celebrations—and the shell is then used as a vessel for a smooth ice cream made from butternut squash.

The contrast between the firmness of the shell and the creamy texture of the vegetable-based ice cream delivers a cooling, comforting experience. Emmanuel playfully uses this technique with a number of fruits.

FROZEN TOMATO WITH TOMATO BASIL SORBET

Prep time: 30 minutes

Cooking time: 10 minutes

Chilling time: 24 hours

Freeze time: 20 minutes after churning

Serves: 8

1 ½ tsp fresh basil

⅓ tsp salt

¼ tsp freshly ground pepper

½ cup + 1 tbsp (120 g) granulated sugar

¼ cup (55 g) inulin

1 tsp sorbet stabilizer

8 tomatoes

FOR SERVING

Fresh basil leaves

1. In a saucepan, bring ¾ cup + 2 tbsp (210 ml) of water to a boil with the basil, salt, and ground pepper. Add the granulated sugar, inulin, and stabilizer. Stir and heat to 212°F (100°C) checking with a probe thermometer.
2. Blend the mixture using an immersion blender and strain through a fine mesh sieve into a heatproof container. Cool rapidly in the freezer to 39°F (4°C).
3. Wash and dry the tomatoes. Cut off the top fourth of each tomato, and set the tops aside. Scoop the flesh out of the tomatoes with a spoon and place in a bowl. You'll need 3 ¼ cups (750 g) of tomato pulp.
4. Place the hollowed tomatoes and their tops on a tray and freeze.
5. Stir the tomato pulp into the chilled mixture.
6. Blend again and refrigerate for 24 hours.
7. Blend once more and churn in an ice cream maker. Freeze for 20 minutes after churning.

PLATING

8. Fill a piping bag fitted with a plain No. 10 tip with the Tomato Basil Sorbet.
9. Pipe the sorbet into the frozen tomato bottoms, place the tops back on, and garnish with basil leaves.

FROZEN BANANA WITH BANANA ICE CREAM AND BANANA CHIPS

Prep time: 40 minutes

Cooking time: 40 minutes

Chilling time: 4 hours

Freeze time: 20 minutes

Serves: 4

2 cups (480 ml) whole milk

¾ cup (180 ml) heavy cream

½ cup (100 g) granulated sugar

3 tbsp atomized glucose

2 tbsp milk powder

½ tsp stabilizer

1 cup (250 g) banana purée

BANANA CHIPS

1 banana

1 tbsp powdered sugar

FOR SERVING

4 small frécinette (or lady finger) bananas

BANANA ICE CREAM

1 In a saucepan, bring the milk and cream to a boil. Add the granulated sugar, atomized glucose, milk powder, and stabilizer.
2 Stir and heat to 185°F (85°C) checking with a probe thermometer.
3 Stir in the banana purée. Using an immersion blender, blend thoroughly, and transfer to a heatproof container. Cool quickly in the freezer to 39°F (4°C).
4 Once cooled, infuse in the refrigerator for 4 hours.
5 Blend again and churn in an ice cream maker.

BANANA CHIPS

6 Preheat the oven to 175°F (80°C). Arrange on a baking sheet lined with parchment paper.
7 Using a vegetable peeler, cut long, thin banana slices. Dust with powdered sugar using a fine sieve. Bake for 30 minutes.
8 Let cool and store in a dry place.

PLATING

9 Cut the small frécinette bananas in half and freeze for at least 20 minutes.
10 Fill a piping bag fitted with a plain No. 8 tip with the banana ice cream.
11 Pipe the ice cream onto the chilled banana halves and freeze for at least 20 minutes. Remove from the freezer 15 minutes before serving. Garnish each frozen banana with a banana chip.

CHEF'S TIP

The combination of the frozen banana and ice cream offers a long-lasting banana flavor.

FROZEN PASSION FRUIT WITH PASSION FRUIT SORBET

Prep time: 30 minutes

Cooking time: 12 minutes

Chilling time: 24 hours

Freeze time: 30 minutes

Serves: 8

2 tbsp invert sugar

⅔ cup (140 g) atomized glucose

1 tsp sorbet stabilizer

2 ¼ cups (540 ml) passion fruit juice

⅔ cup (160 ml) mango purée

FOR SERVING

8 passion fruits

PASSION FRUIT SORBET

1. In a saucepan, bring ¾ cup + 2 tbsp (210 ml) of water and invert sugar to a boil. Add the atomized glucose and stabilizer.
2. Heat to 212°F (100°C) checking with a probe thermometer, then blend with an immersion blender.
3. Let the syrup cool to room temperature, then stir in the passion fruit juice and mango purée.
4. Mix thoroughly, blend again, and infuse in the refrigerator for 24 hours.
5. Blend again and churn in an ice cream maker.

PLATING

6. Clean the passion fruits thoroughly. Cut off the top fourth of each passion fruit, saving the tops. Scoop the pulp out of each fruit with a spoon.
7. Freeze the emptied fruit shells and their tops.
8. Fill a piping bag fitted with a plain No. 8 tip with the passion fruit sorbet.
9. Fill the frozen shells and replace the tops.

CHEF'S TIP

Save the seeds from the passion fruits and mix them into the sorbet after churning.

FROZEN MINI HALLOWEEN SQUASH

Prep time: 40 minutes

Cook time: 50 minutes

Chill time: 24 hours

Freeze time: 40 minutes

Serves: 8

BUTTERNUT SQUASH PURÉE

11 ½ oz (325 g) butternut squash

3 tbsp granulated sugar

HALLOWEEN ICE CREAM

1 vanilla bean

2 cups (480 ml) whole milk

¾ cup (180 ml) heavy cream

1 tsp ground ginger

⅛ tsp ground cinnamon

⅛ tsp ground turmeric

⅛ tsp salt

½ cup + 1 tbsp (110 g) granulated sugar

½ cup (105 g) atomized glucose

½ cup (60 g) nonfat dry milk

1 ¼ tsp ice cream stabilizer

1 cup (250 g) squash purée (recipe following)

FOR SERVING

8 mini pumpkins (pomarine or Jack-be-little variety)

BUTTERNUT SQUASH PURÉE

1. Peel the squash and cut it into chunks. In a saucepan, bring 2 cups (480 ml) of water to a boil, add the squash, and cook for 40 minutes until tender.
2. Drain and blend the cooked squash with the sugar using an immersion blender. Set aside.

HALLOWEEN ICE CREAM

3. Split the vanilla pod in half and scrape out the seeds. In a saucepan, bring the milk, cream, vanilla pod and seeds, spices, and salt to a boil. Stir in the sugar, atomized glucose, dry milk, and stabilizer. Stir and heat to 185°F (85°C), checking with a probe thermometer.
4. Strain through a fine mesh sieve, removing the vanilla pod. Off the heat, stir in 1 cup (240 ml) of the squash purée.
5. Using an immersion blender, blend the mixture and then transfer to a heatproof container. Chill rapidly in the freezer to 39°F (4°C).
6. Once cold, refrigerate for 24 hours to infuse.
7. Blend again and churn in an ice cream maker.

PLATING

8. Clean the mini pumpkins and slice off the top third of each to make lids.
9. Scoop out the centers using a tablespoon. Freeze the shells and lids for 30 minutes before serving.
10. Fill a piping bag fitted with a plain No. 8 tip with the Halloween Ice Cream.
11. Pipe the ice cream into the squash shells and return to the freezer for 10 minutes. Place the lids on before serving.

FROZEN PINEAPPLE WITH SORBET AND CARAMELIZED BANANAS

Prep time: 1 ½ hours

Cook time: 12 minutes

Chill time: 24 hours

Freeze time: 20 minutes after churning

Serves: 8

VICTORIA PINEAPPLE SORBET

3 tbsp granulated sugar

2 tbsp atomized glucose

½ tsp sorbet stabilizer

4 Victoria pineapples

2 tbsp lemon juice

COCONUT SORBET

1 cup (200 g) granulated sugar

2 tbsp atomized glucose

1 ½ tsp sorbet stabilizer

4 ¼ cups (1 kg) sweetened coconut purée

CARAMELIZED BANANAS

2 tbsp butter

2 tbsp granulated sugar

1 ⅓ cups (200 g) bananas, sliced

½ tsp ground nutmeg

2 tsp Mount Gay rum

FOR SERVING

Coconut flakes

PINEAPPLE SORBET

1 In a saucepan, bring 3 tbsp of water to a boil. Add the sugar, atomized glucose, and stabilizer. Stir and heat to 212°F (100°C), checking with a probe thermometer.

2 Cut the pineapples in half lengthwise, keeping the leaves attached. Hollow them out and measure out 1 ¾ cups (250 g) of pineapple flesh. Freeze the shells for at least 30 minutes.

3 Add the pineapple flesh and lemon juice.

4 Using an immersion blender, blend and then strain through a fine mesh sieve. Transfer to a heatproof container and chill rapidly in the freezer to 39°F (4°C), then refrigerate for 24 hours to infuse.

5 Blend again and churn.

COCONUT SORBET

6 Bring ¾ cup + 2 tbsp (210 ml) of water to a boil in a saucepan. Add the sugar, atomized glucose, and stabilizer. Stir and heat to 212°F (100°C).

7 Pour over the coconut purée. Blend using an immersion blender, transfer to a heatproof container, and chill rapidly in the freezer to 39°F (4°C). Infuse for at least 4 hours in the refrigerator.

8 Blend again and churn.

CARAMELIZED BANANAS

9 In a skillet, melt the butter with the sugar. Add sliced bananas and nutmeg. Cook briefly to retain a firm texture, then flambé with the rum. Set aside.

PLATING

10 Pipe the pineapple sorbet using a piping bag fitting with a plain No. 10 tip halfway into the frozen shells. Add caramelized bananas, top with more pineapple sorbet, and freeze again until serving.

11 Pipe the coconut sorbet on top using another piping bag fitted with a plain No. 10 tip. Garnish with coconut flakes.

CHEF'S TIP

If possible, use Victoria pineapples from Réunion Island for the ideal size and perfect flavor balance.

FROZEN YUZU WITH CANDIED YUZU AND YUZU ICE CREAM

Prep time: 40 minutes

Candying time: 3 days

Cook time: 45 minutes

Chill time: 4 hours

Freeze time: 30 minutes

Serves: 5

CANDIED YUZU:

5 large yuzus

3 ¼ cups (750 g) granulated sugar, divided

YUZU ICE CREAM:

2 cups (480 ml) whole milk

¾ cup + 1 tbsp (195 ml) heavy cream

½ cup (100 g) granulated sugar

⅓ cup (80 g) atomized glucose

½ cup (50 g) nonfat dry milk

1 tsp ice cream stabilizer

¼ cup (60 ml) yuzu juice

CANDIED YUZU

1 Wash the yuzus and slice off the top quarter of each fruit. Scoop out the insides and reserve the pulp for another use. Blanch the hollowed-out yuzus and tops by boiling them for 1 minute in 3 ¼ cups (780 ml) of water. Repeat this blanching step three times using fresh water each time.

2 Place the blanched yuzus in a saucepan with the water and 1 ⅓ cups (250 g) of the sugar. Bring to a boil, then let cool overnight.

3 The next day, heat the syrup with the yuzus, add another 1 ⅓ cups (250 g) sugar, and bring to a boil. Cool overnight again. On the third day, repeat the heating with the remaining sugar.

4 Let cool to room temperature, then refrigerate.

YUZU ICE CREAM

5 In a saucepan, bring the milk and cream to a boil. Add the sugar, atomized glucose, dry milk, and stabilizer.

6 Stir and heat to 185°F (85°C), checking with a probe thermometer.

7 Using an immersion blender, blend the mixture and transfer to a heatproof container. Chill quickly in the freezer to 39°F (4°C).

8 Stir in the yuzu juice, then let infuse in the refrigerator for at least 4 hours.

9 Blend again and churn.

ASSEMBLY

10 Drain the candied yuzu shells on a wire rack. Freeze them for 20 minutes.

11 Fill a piping bag fitted with a plain No. 8 tip with the yuzu ice cream.

12 Pipe the ice cream into the yuzu shells. Freeze for 10 minutes before serving.

CHEF'S TIP

Opt for organic yuzu whenever possible. You can skip the candying step for a quicker version, but going through the full process brings out intense flavor and a refreshingly vibrant finish. Reserve the yuzu syrup for flavoring fruit salad, soaking cakes, or even just stirring into plain yogurt.

POPSICLES, GRANITAS & FROZEN YOGURTS

Unlike travel cakes or fruit-stuffed frozen desserts, these frozen treats are a grown-up twist on childhood delights. Take the popsicles, which are crafted like cocktails and melt smoothly on your tongue. Emmanuel uses only a touch of ice to preserve the cocktail experience, whether it's a Campari mix, a splash of pastis, or a mojito base, so enjoy responsibly.

The pastis cocktail popsicle is a nod to the classic French drink, and Emmanuel calls it an "apéritif on a stick." Consider pairing it with peanuts, which go surprisingly well with the popsicle's licorice and anise flavors.

EXOTIC POPSICLES

Prep time: 40 minutes

Chill time: 4 hours

Freeze time: At least 4 hours

Serves: 10

COCONUT ICE CREAM

1 cup (240 ml) whole milk

⅔ cup (160 ml) heavy cream

¾ cup (160 ml) sweetened coconut purée

⅓ cup (80 g) granulated sugar

2 tbsp atomized glucose

¼ cup (35 g) skim milk powder

½ tsp sorbet stabilizer

TROPICAL COULIS

⅓ cup (80 ml) mango purée

2 tbsp passion fruit juice

2 tsp ginger juice

3 tbsp granulated sugar

1 tsp orange blossom honey

CRUNCHY WHITE COATING

2.2 lb (1 kg) white chocolate

⅓ cup (100 g) cocoa butter

Shredded coconut

COCONUT ICE CREAM

1 In a saucepan, bring the milk, cream, and coconut purée to a boil. In a bowl, mix together the sugar, glucose, milk powder, and stabilizer, then add to the pan.

2 Heat everything to 185°F (85°C), checking with a probe thermometer.

3 Using an immersion blender, blend and then transfer to a heatproof container. Cool rapidly in the freezer to 39°F (4°C).

4 Let infuse in the refrigerator for at least 4 hours.

5 Blend again and churn in an ice cream maker.

TROPICAL COULIS

6 In a saucepan, gently heat all the ingredients to 86°F (30°C).

7 Let the coulis cool.

ASSEMBLY

8 Place popsicle molds in the freezer until chilled.

9 Transfer the coconut ice cream to a piping bag and fill each mold halfway, spreading it up the sides. Insert the sticks.

10 Freeze for 15 minutes.

11 Pour 2 tsp of coulis into the center of each mold. Freeze for 20 minutes.

12 Top with more coconut ice cream and freeze for at least 3 hours.

CRUNCHY WHITE COATING

13 In a saucepan, gently melt the white chocolate and cocoa butter to 104°F (40°C).

14 Unmold the popsicles and dip them into the coating, then quickly roll them in shredded coconut. Either serve immediately or refreeze on a plate.

CHEF'S TIP

For best results, dip the popsicles while they're fully frozen and the coating is at 104°F (40°C). If the coating is too cold, it will set too thick.

CAMPARI COCKTAIL POPSICLES

Prep time: 20 minutes

Cook time: 10 minutes

Chill time: 4 hours

Freeze time: At least 12 hours

Serves: 10

½ cup (100 g) granulated sugar

3 tbsp atomized glucose

½ tsp sorbet stabilizer

1 cup (240 ml) passion fruit juice

½ cup (120 ml) Campari

1. In a saucepan, bring 1 cup (240 ml) of water to a boil with the granulated sugar, atomized glucose, and stabilizer.
2. Stir and bring the mixture to 212°F (100°C), checking with a probe thermometer.
3. Using an immersion blender, blend the mixture. Transfer to a heatproof container and cool quickly in the freezer to 39°F (4°C). Add the passion fruit juice and Campari.
4. Let infuse for at least 4 hours in the refrigerator.
5. Blend the infusion again and churn in an ice cream maker.

ASSEMBLY

6. Place the popsicle molds in the freezer until chilled.
7. Transfer the Campari sorbet to a piping bag and fill the molds halfway. Insert the sticks, then finish filling the molds with the sorbet and smooth the surface.
8. Return the filled molds to the freezer for at least 12 hours before unmolding.

PASTIS COCKTAIL POPSICLES

Prep time: 20 minutes

Cook time: 10 minutes

Chill time: 4 hours

Freeze time: At least 12 hours

Serves: 10

PASTIS SORBET

½ cup (105 g) granulated sugar

¼ cup (60 g) atomized glucose

1 tsp sorbet stabilizer

3 tbsp pastis

1 In a saucepan, bring 2 ¾ cups (660 ml) of water to a boil with the granulated sugar, atomized glucose, and stabilizer.
2 Stir and bring the mixture to 212°F (100°C), checking with a probe thermometer.
3 Using an immersion blender, blend the mixture. Transfer to a heatproof container and cool quickly in the freezer to 39°F (4°C). Add the pastis.
4 Let infuse for 4 hours in the refrigerator.
5 Blend the infusion again and churn in an ice cream maker.

ASSEMBLY

6 Place the popsicle molds in the freezer until chilled.
7 Transfer the pastis sorbet to a piping bag and fill the molds halfway. Insert the sticks, then finish filling with more sorbet, smoothing the top.
8 Return the molds to the freezer for at least 12 hours before unmolding.

COCKTAIL
VERMOUTH
VERMOUTH

MOJITO COCKTAIL POPSICLES

Prep time: 20 minutes

Cook time: 10 minutes

Chill time: 24 hours

Freeze time: At least 12 hours

Serves: 10

Zest of 2 limes
2 tbsp fresh mint leaves
⅔ cup (130 g) light brown sugar
⅓ cup (80 g) atomized glucose
1 tsp sorbet stabilizer
1 cup (240 ml) lime juice
7 tbsp white rum

1. In a saucepan, bring 1 ⅔ cups (400 ml) of water to a boil with the lime zest and mint leaves. Add the brown sugar, atomized glucose, and stabilizer.
2. Stir and bring the mixture to 212°F (100°C), checking with a probe thermometer.
3. Using an immersion blender, blend the mixture. Transfer to a heatproof container, and cool quickly in the freezer to 39°F (4°C), then add the lime juice and white rum.
4. Let infuse for 24 hours in the refrigerator.
5. Strain through a chinois strainer, blend again, and churn in an ice cream maker.

ASSEMBLY

6. Place the popsicle molds in the freezer until chilled.
7. Transfer the mojito sorbet to a piping bag and fill the molds halfway. Insert the sticks, then finish filling and smooth the top.
8. Return the molds to the freezer for at least 12 hours before unmolding.

CLAIRETTE DE DIE MUSCAT AND STRAWBERRY GRANITA

Prep time: 20 minutes

Cook time: 5 minutes

Freeze time: 3 hours

Serves: 8

1 cup (200 g) granulated sugar

1 bottle of Clairette de Die Muscat

1 ¾ lb (800 g) fresh strawberries, hulled and sliced thinly

FOR SERVING

Dried rose petals

1. In a large saucepan, bring 1 ¼ cups (300 ml) of water and the sugar to a boil. Let the syrup cool, stir in the Clairette, and transfer to a container. Place in the freezer.
2. Whisk the mixture occasionally to create a snow-like texture. Keep frozen until ready to serve (at least 3 hours).

PLATING

3. Line the insides of serving glasses with the strawberry slices to create a floral pattern. Refrigerate until needed.
4. Scoop the Clairette granita into each glass. Garnish with a few dried rose petals.

COCONUT FROZEN YOGURT WITH TROPICAL SAUCE

Prep time: 30 minutes

Cook time: 15 minutes

Chill time: 4 hours

Freeze time: 10 minutes

Serves: 8

COCONUT FROZEN YOGURT

1½ tbsp coconut cream

⅓ cup (80 g) granulated sugar

½ cup (110 g) atomized glucose

1 tsp ice cream stabilizer

1 ¼ cups (300 g) plain yogurt

TROPICAL COULIS

½ cup (100 g) granulated sugar

1 ⅓ cups (200 g) mango flesh

⅓ cup (80 ml) passion fruit juice

1 tsp ginger juice

COCONUT FROZEN YOGURT

1. In a saucepan, bring 1 cup (240 ml) of water and the coconut cream to a boil. Add the sugar, glucose, and stabilizer. Stir and heat to 212°F (100°C).
2. Using an immersion blender, blend the mixture. Transfer to a heatproof container and cool rapidly in the freezer to 39°F (4°C). Add the yogurt.
3. Blend again and let it infuse in the refrigerator for at least 4 hours.
4. Blend one last time and churn in an ice cream maker.

TROPICAL COULIS

5. In a saucepan, bring ½ cup (120 ml) of water and the sugar to a boil.
6. Pour the syrup over the chopped mango. Add the passion fruit juice and ginger juice. Blend and set aside.

PLATING

7. Place shallow bowls in the freezer.
8. Transfer the coconut yogurt to a piping bag fitted with a plain No. 8 tip.
9. Pipe into the frozen bowls and return to the freezer for at least 10 minutes.
10. Just before serving, spoon the tropical coulis over the frozen yogurt.

FROZEN SHEEP'S MILK YOGURT WITH RED BERRY COULIS

Prep time: 30 minutes

Cook time: 15 minutes

Chill time: 24 hours

Freeze time: 10 minutes

Serves: 8

FROZEN YOGURT

⅓ cup (75 g) granulated sugar

½ cup (110 g) atomized glucose

1 tsp ice cream stabilizer

1 ⅓ cups (330 g) sheep's milk yogurt

RED BERRY COULIS

½ cup (100 g) granulated sugar

1 tsp fresh mint leaves

1 ⅓ cups (200 g) strawberries, ideally Mara des Bois

¾ cup (100 g) raspberries

FROZEN YOGURT

1. In a saucepan, bring 1 cup (240 ml) of water to a boil, then add the granulated sugar, atomized glucose, and stabilizer. Stir and bring to 212°F (100°C), checking with a probe thermometer.
2. Using an immersion blender, blend the mixture. Transfer to a heatproof container. Let cool quickly in the freezer to 39°F (4°C), then incorporate the sheep's milk yogurt.
3. Blend again and allow to infuse in the refrigerator for 24 hours.
4. Blend once more and churn in an ice cream maker.

RED BERRY COULIS

5. In a saucepan, bring ½ cup (120 ml) of water, the sugar, and mint to a boil. Using an immersion blender, blend this syrup and strain through a chinois strainer.
6. Pour over the red berries and blend again. Set aside.

PLATING

7. Place empty glass yogurt pots in the freezer.
8. Transfer the frozen yogurt to a piping bag fitted with a plain No. 8 tip.
9. Fill the frozen jars leaving about an inch space at the top using the piping bag and return them to the freezer for 10 minutes.
10. Just before serving, add the red berry coulis.

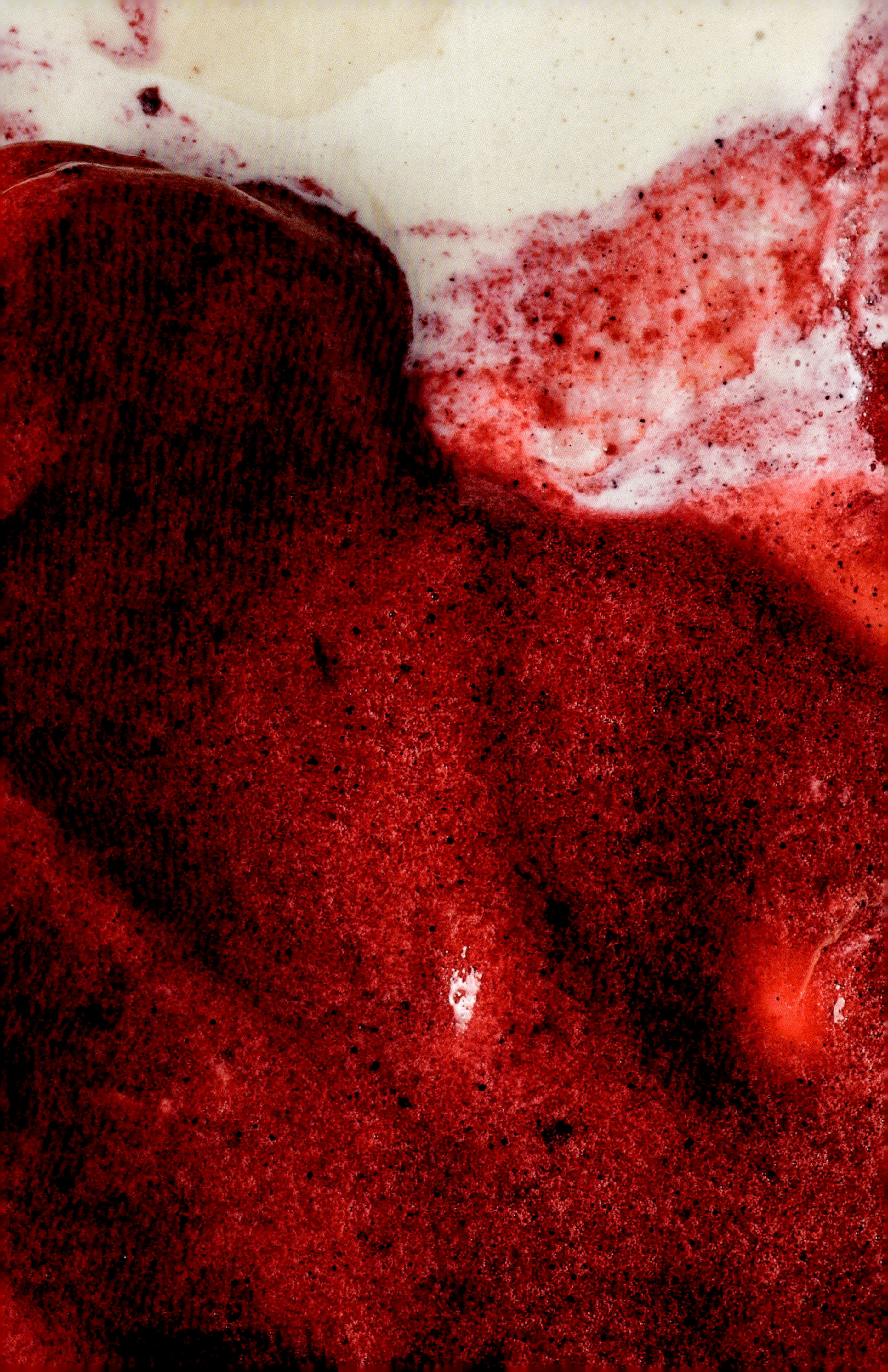

FROZEN DESSERTS

Emmanuel has always enjoyed reimagining classic frozen desserts. Semifreddo, tiramisu, frozen nougats, and crêpes are among the many treats he likes to break down, reinvent, and pair with unexpected flavors to create new tasting experiences.

The semifreddo, a staple of Italian pastry, is essential to any ice cream maker's repertoire and can be prepared at home without any complicated equipment. Traditionally made with a blend of Italian meringue and whipped cream, it lends itself to endless variations. Emmanuel's takes include ice cream bases flavored with chocolate, nuts, or a splash of whisky to bring out the aromas and deepen the flavors.

Inspired by a trip to Provence, Emmanuel's Raspberry Frozen Nougat is rich, refreshing, and crunchy. This indulgent dessert, made with sugar, almonds, honey, egg whites, vanilla, and pistachios, highlights the aromatic notes of the region.

In a very different approach to frozen dessert, Emmanuel created a Beet Soup with Green Apple Sorbet. Through this pairing, he aims to turn the humble beet—one of his favorite vegetables—into something truly indulgent. Lemon jelly and green apple sorbet awaken and brighten the beet's natural earthiness. Typically enjoyed in summer, this dish perfectly illustrates the kind of sensory experimentation Emmanuel pursues. He loves surprising the palate and offering a fresh take on familiar and sometimes overlooked ingredients.

Crêpe Suzette, that great French classic, also captured Emmanuel's creative attention. Allegedly invented at the end of the nineteenth century by Chef Auguste Escoffier for the future King of England during a stay in Monaco, this dessert is the basis for a whole collection of recipes in Emmanuel's kitchen. He prepares his version with a gluten-free batter made from rice flour, which creates a lace-like effect when cooked. He pairs it with yuzu, a citrus fruit of Chinese origin now found across the globe. This combination produces a delicately perfumed crêpe with a subtle, refreshing flavor. Traditionally served at the end of a meal, this dessert is enjoyable year-round—at breakfast, at lunch, in the afternoon with coffee or hot chocolate, or even better, with a fine cup of tea.

FROSTED LEMON

Prep time: 40 minutes

Cook time: 45 minutes

Chill time: 4 hours

Candied lemon prep: 3 days

Freeze time: 30 minutes

Serves: 5

CANDIED LEMONS

- 5 large lemons
- 3 ¾ cups (750 g) granulated sugar, divided

LEMON SORBET

- 1 ¼ cups (240 g) granulated sugar
- ¾ cup (110 g) atomized glucose
- 1 tsp sorbet stabilizer
- 1 ¼ cups (300 ml) lemon juice
- Pulp from 1 lemon

FOR SERVING

- Edible silver leaf

CANDIED LEMONS

1. Wash the lemons and cut off the top fourth of each. Scoop the pulp out of each lemon, reserving it for the sorbet. Blanch the empty lemon shells and tops for 1 minute by boiling them in water, then repeat the process three times, each time with fresh water.
2. Place the blanched lemons in a saucepan with 3 ¼ cups (780 ml) of water and 1 ¼ cup (250 g) of the sugar. Bring to a boil, then let the mixture cool overnight.
3. The next day, reheat the syrup with the lemons. Add another 1 ¼ cups (250 g) of the sugar and bring to a boil again. Let cool overnight.
4. On the third day, repeat the same process with the remaining sugar. Let the lemons cool to room temperature, then refrigerate.

LEMON SORBET

5. In a saucepan, bring 1 ¼ cups (300 ml) of water to a boil. Add the sugar, atomized glucose, and stabilizer. Stir and bring to 212°F (100°C), checking with a probe thermometer.
6. Add the lemon juice, lemon pulp and, using an immersion blender, blend the mixture. Strain it through a fine mesh sieve or chinois strainer.
7. Transfer to a heatproof container, and cool quickly in the freezer to 39°F (4°C), then let it rest for at least 4 hours in the refrigerator.
8. Blend again, then churn in an ice cream maker.

PLATING

9. Drain the candied lemon shells and tops on a wire rack. Place them in the freezer for 20 minutes.
10. Fill a piping bag fitted with a plain No. 8 tip with the lemon sorbet.
11. Pipe the sorbet into the lemon shells, creating a rounded dome on top. Freeze the filled lemons for 10 minutes.
12. Garnish with small discs cut from the candied lemon tops and a touch of edible silver leaf.

CHEF'S TIP

Organic lemons work best for this recipe.

If you want to simplify the process, you can skip the candying step, but the slow infusion of lemon into the simple syrup adds depth and brightness.

Save the leftover syrup to flavor fruit salad or soak pound cake. The citrus aroma will be wonderfully intense.

FROZEN COINTREAU SOUFFLÉ

Prep time: 1 hour 30 minutes

Cook time: 30 minutes

Freeze time: 4 hours

Serves: 8

ORANGE SEGMENTS

2 oranges

COINTREAU SOUFFLÉ

2 ½ tsp powdered gelatin

⅔ cup (130 g) granulated sugar

5 egg yolks

1 ¾ cups (400 g) premade whipped cream

2 tbsp Cointreau

JAPANESE SPONGE CAKE

4 egg whites

½ tsp cream of tartar

½ cup + 2 tsp (120 g) granulated sugar, divided

2 eggs

⅛ tsp salt

2 tbsp grapeseed oil

¾ cup (100 g) all-purpose flour

1 ½ tsp baking powder

COINTREAU SYRUP:

½ cup (100 g) granulated sugar

3 tbsp + 1 tsp Cointreau

ORANGE SEGMENTS

1 Peel the oranges with a knife, removing all the white pith. Cut out the segments and set aside.

COINTREAU SOUFFLÉ

2 In a small bowl, bloom the gelatin in 2 to 3 tbsp of cold water for 5 to 10 minutes.

3 In a saucepan, heat 3 tbsp of water and the sugar to 240°F (116°C), checking with a probe thermometer. Pour over the egg yolks while whisking constantly.

4 Continue cooking the mixture in a double boiler until it reaches 181°F (83°C). Add the bloomed gelatin to the double boiler and stir.

5 Transfer the mixture to a stand mixer and blend until it has cooled completely. Gently fold in the whipped cream and Cointreau. Set aside.

JAPANESE SPONGE CAKE

6 Place the egg whites and cream of tartar in a mixing bowl and chill in the freezer for 10 minutes.

7 Preheat the oven to 400°F (200°C).

8 Whip the chilled egg whites, cream of tartar, and ⅓ cup + 2 tsp (85 g) sugar until stiff peaks form.

9 In another bowl, whisk the remaining 2 tbsp sugar with the whole eggs, salt, and grapeseed oil. In a separate bowl, sift together the flour and baking powder, then fold into the egg mixture.

10 Fold in the whipped egg whites gently with a spatula.

11 Pour the batter into a 13-inch (33-cm) square Flexipan mold. Lower the oven to 360°F (180°C) and bake until golden, 18 to 20 minutes.

12 After baking, place a sheet of parchment paper on top of the cake, turn it over, and let it cool.

COINTREAU SYRUP

13 In a saucepan, bring ½ cup (120 ml) of water and the sugar to a boil. Remove from heat and let cool slightly. Stir in the Cointreau and set aside. (This syrup is brushed over the sponge cake before assembling the soufflé to keep the cake moist and infuse it with flavor.)

ASSEMBLY

14 Cut out 16 rounds of sponge using a 2 ½ in (6 cm) cookie cutter. Soak them with the Cointreau syrup.

15 Place a tart ring 1 in (2.5 cm) high and 3 ¼ in (8 cm) in diameter inside each ramekin of the same size. Set one soaked Japanese sponge round at the bottom.

16 Transfer the Cointreau ice cream to a piping bag fitted with a plain No. 8 tip. Pipe it halfway up the ramekin, then add a second soaked sponge round.

17 Finish filling with the Cointreau ice cream to the top edge of the ring. Smooth the surface with an offset spatula and place in the freezer for 15 minutes.

FINISHING

18 Just before serving, slightly warm the tart ring to remove it.

19 Caramelize the orange sections with a kitchen torch and arrange them neatly on top of the frozen soufflé.

POACHED PEAR WITH PEAR SORBET

Prep time: 1 hour

Cook time: 30 minutes

Rest time: 24 hours

Chill time: 4 hours

Freeze time: 20 minutes after churning

Serves: 8

POACHED PEARS

Juice from ½ lemon

Ice cubes

2 ½ cups (500 g) granulated sugar

4 yellow-red Williams pears, peeled, stems intact

COCOA CRUMBLE

3 ½ tbsp butter, softened

¼ cup + 1 tbsp (60 g) granulated sugar

½ cup (60 g) all-purpose flour

1 tbsp unsweetened cocoa powder

PEAR SORBET

⅓ cup + 1 tbsp (77 g) granulated sugar

2 tbsp atomized glucose

½ tsp sorbet stabilizer

3 cups (600 g) peeled and chopped pears

1 ½ tsp pear liqueur

FOR SERVING

Edible gold leaf

POACHED PEARS

1 Fill a bowl with cold water, lemon juice, and ice cubes. Submerge the pears in the lemon water and set aside.

2 In one saucepan, heat 2 cups (480 ml) of water over medium heat. In another saucepan, slowly dry cook the sugar (don't stir) until it turns to an amber caramel. Carefully pour the hot water over the caramel, stir, and set aside.

3 Place the pears in a pot, pour in enough caramel to reach halfway up the fruit, and bring to a gentle simmer. Remove from the heat and cool.

4 Cover with plastic wrap and refrigerate the pears in the caramel for 24 hours. They should be tender but not overcooked.

COCOA CRUMBLE

5 Preheat the oven to 310°F (155°C), using the convection setting.

6 In the bowl of a stand mixer, cream together the butter and sugar. Sift in the flour and cocoa powder, then combine to form a crumbly texture.

7 Spread onto a parchment-lined baking sheet and bake for 12 minutes. Cool and store in a dry place.

PEAR SORBET

8 In a saucepan, bring ¼ cup + 2 tsp (70 ml) of water to a boil. Add the sugar, glucose, and stabilizer. Stir and heat the mixture to 212°F (100°C), checking with a probe thermometer.

9 Using an immersion blender, blend the mixture and then transfer to a heatproof container. Cool it rapidly in the freezer to 39°F (4°C).

10 Place the peeled and chopped pears in a blender and puree them. Add to the syrup along with the pear liqueur. Mix well.

11 Let chill in the refrigerator for 4 hours. Blend again and churn in the ice cream maker. Freeze for 20 minutes after churning.

PLATING

12 In each dish, place half a poached pear. Add 1 tbsp of cocoa crumble and top with a scoop of pear sorbet. Finish with a touch of edible gold leaf.

CHOCOLATE SEMIFREDDO

Prep time: 1 hour 30 minutes

Cook time: 15 minutes

Freeze time: At least 4 hours

Serves: 6

CHOCOLATE PARFAIT

4 oz (110 g) 75 percent cacao Tanzanian chocolate

6 tbsp granulated sugar

4 egg yolks

1 ¼ cups (300 ml) heavy cream, cold

LIGHT CHOCOLATE SPONGE CAKE

4 egg whites

½ tsp cream of tartar

½ cup + 2 tbsp (120 g) granulated sugar, divided

1 egg

¾ tsp salt

2 tbsp grapeseed oil

½ cup (70 g) all-purpose flour

¼ cup (30 g) unsweetened cocoa powder

¾ tsp baking powder

2 tsp softened butter, for greasing the mold

COGNAC SYRUP

¼ cup (50 g) granulated sugar

2 tbsp Rémy Martin cognac

FOR SERVING

75 percent cacao Tanzanian chocolate

CHOCOLATE PARFAIT

1 Melt the chocolate in a double boiler.

2 In a saucepan, bring 2 tbsp of water and the sugar to 240°F (116°C) checking with a probe thermometer.

3 Pour over the egg yolks and beat with an electric mixer until completely cool. Add the melted chocolate and mix well.

4 Whip the cold cream to soft peaks and gently fold it into the chocolate mixture. Set aside.

LIGHT CHOCOLATE SPONGE CAKE

5 Place the egg whites in a stand mixer bowl and freeze for 10 minutes. Whip the chilled egg whites with the cream of tartar and 6 tbsp sugar until stiff peaks form.

6 In a mixing bowl, whisk the whole egg (do not whip), the remaining sugar, salt, and oil. Sift in the flour, cocoa powder, and baking powder, and mix to combine.

7 Gently fold the whipped egg whites into this mixture using a spatula.

8 Preheat the oven to 360°F (180°C) with the convection setting.

9 Butter a 12-inch (30-cm) square frame with softened butter and place it on a baking tray lined with a nonstick baking mat. Pour in the batter.

10 Place the tray in the oven and immediately reduce the temperature to 290°F (145°C). Bake for 9 minutes.

11 Remove from the oven, place a sheet of parchment over the sponge cake, flip it over, and let cool.

COGNAC SYRUP

12 In a saucepan, heat ¼ cup (60 ml) of water and the sugar to 122°F (50°C). Let cool, then add the cognac and mix.

ASSEMBLY

13 Peel the baking mat off of the sponge cake. Cut six 1-by-7 ¼-inch (5-by-18.5 cm) strips of sponge cake and set aside.

14 Cut out twelve 1 ¾-inch (4.5-cm) rounds with a cookie cutter. Soak them in the cognac syrup.

15 Line six 2 ½-inch (6-cm) diameter and 2-inch (5-cm) high stainless steel rings with acetate strips. Place acetate discs at the bottom. (Lining the stainless steel rings with these flexible plastic strips allows you to unmold your semifreddo easily.)

16 Line the inside of each ring with a strip of sponge cake, and place a soaked sponge cake round at the bottom.

17 Fill a piping bag fitted with a plain round No. 8 tip with the chocolate parfait. Pipe the parfait halfway up each ring, insert another soaked sponge round, and finish piping the parfait in a dome shape. Freeze for at least 4 hours.

PLATING

18 Unmold and remove the acetate strips.

19 Use a vegetable peeler to make chocolate curls and place them on top of the semifreddo.

CHEF'S TIP

To ensure perfect texture, transfer the desserts to the refrigerator for 15 minutes before serving.

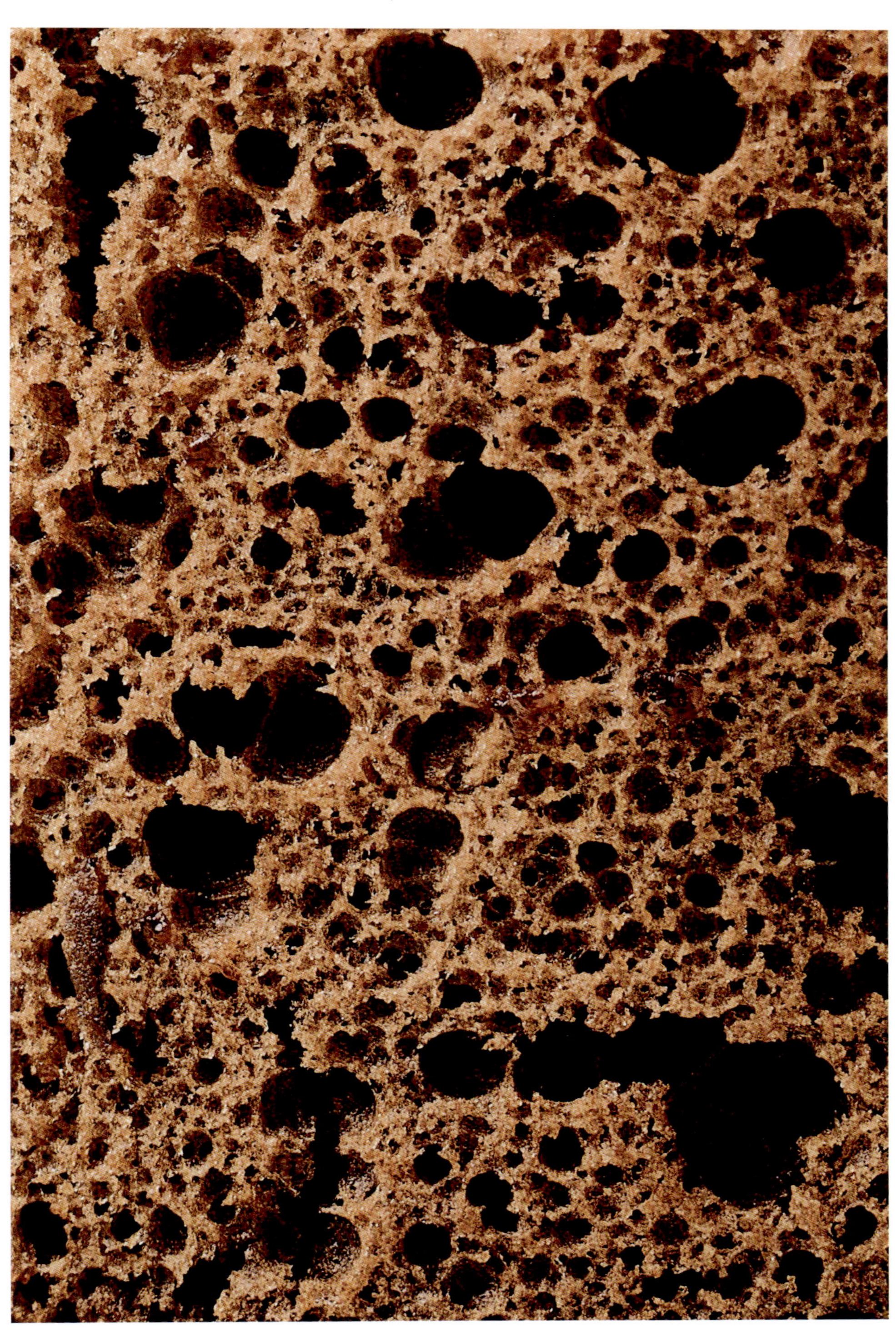

CHESTNUT SEMIFREDDO

Prep time: 1 hour 30 minutes

Cook time: 15 minutes

Freeze time: At least 4 hours

Serves: 6

CHESTNUT PARFAIT

½ cup (100 g) granulated sugar

5 egg yolks

3 tbsp chestnut cream

5 tbsp chestnut purée

¾ cup + 1 tbsp (195 ml) heavy cream, cold

LIGHT CHESTNUT SPONGE CAKE

2 tsp softened butter, for the mold

4 egg whites

½ tsp cream of tartar

½ cup + 2 tbsp (120 g) granulated sugar

1 egg

¾ tsp salt

2 tbsp grapeseed oil

¾ cup (100 g) chestnut flour

¾ tsp baking powder

DARK RUM SYRUP

¼ cup (50 g) granulated sugar

2 tbsp Mount Gay dark rum

FOR SERVING

Cooked chestnuts

Unsweetened cocoa powder

Edible gold leaf (optional)

CHESTNUT PARFAIT

1 In a saucepan, heat 3 tbsp of water and the sugar to 240°F (116°C) checking with a probe thermometer.

2 Pour over the egg yolks and whip with an electric mixer until fully cooled.

3 Mix the chestnut cream and chestnut purée together, then fold into the egg mixture.

4 Whip the cold cream to soft peaks and gently fold it into the mixture. Set aside.

LIGHT CHESTNUT SPONGE CAKE

5 Preheat the oven to 360°F (180°C) using the convection setting. Grease a 12-inch (30-cm) square frame with butter and place it on a tray lined with a nonstick baking mat.

6 Place the egg whites in the mixer bowl and freeze for 10 minutes. Whip with the cream of tartar and 6 tbsp sugar until stiff peaks form.

7 In a separate bowl, whisk the egg (do not whip), the remaining sugar, salt, and oil. Sift in the chestnut flour and baking powder, and mix until smooth.

8 Gently fold the egg whites into the mixture with a spatula. Pour the batter into the prepared cake pan.

9 Place the tray in the oven and immediately reduce the temperature to 290°F (145°C). Bake for 9 minutes.

10 Remove from the oven, place a sheet of parchment over the sponge cake, flip it, and let cool.

DARK RUM SYRUP

11 In a saucepan, heat ¼ cup (60 ml) of water and the sugar to 122°F (50°C). Let cool, then add the rum and mix.

ASSEMBLY

12 Peel the baking mat off of the chestnut sponge cake. Cut six 2-inch-by-7¼-inch (5-by-18.5 cm) strips. Cut out twelve 1 ¾-inch (4.5-cm) rounds with a cookie cutter. Soak the rounds in the rum syrup.

13 Line six 2 ½-inch (6-cm) diameter and 2-inch (5-cm) high stainless steel rings with acetate strips and place acetate discs at the bottom. (Lining the stainless steel rings with these flexible plastic strips allows you to unmold your semifreddo easily.)

14 Line the rings with the sponge cake strips and place a soaked sponge cake round at the bottom.

15 Fill a piping bag fitted with a plain No. 8 tip with the chestnut parfait. Pipe the parfait halfway up the rings, add another soaked sponge round, then finish piping the parfait in a dome shape. Freeze for at least 4 hours.

PLATING

16 Unmold and remove the acetate strips.

17 Use a mandoline to shave thin slices of cooked chestnut and arrange on the semifreddo. Using a pastry scraper dipped in cocoa powder, add decorative lines to the sponge base and (optional) edible gold leaf.

CHEF'S TIP

As with the previous version, to ensure perfect texture, transfer the desserts to the refrigerator for 15 minutes before serving.

COCONUT SEMIFREDDO

Prep time: 1 hour 30 minutes

Cook time: 20 minutes

Freeze time: at least 20 hours

Serves: 6

COCONUT PARFAIT

½ cup (120 ml) coconut purée

3 egg yolks

7 tbsp granulated sugar

1 cup (240 ml) heavy cream, cold

ALMOND COCONUT SPONGE CAKE

5 egg whites

½ tsp cream of tartar

3 tbsp granulated sugar

2 eggs

⅔ cup (80 g) powdered sugar

¾ cup (80 g) almond flour

1 tbsp butter, melted

3 tbsp all-purpose flour

½ cup (50 g) shredded coconut

COCONUT COULIS

2 tsp powdered gelatin

1 ¼ cups (300 ml) coconut purée

Zest of 1 lime

1 ½ tsp Malibu rum

FOR SERVING

Coconut shavings

COCONUT PARFAIT

1 In a saucepan, bring the coconut purée to a boil.

2 In a mixing bowl, whisk the egg yolks with the sugar until pale and fluffy. Add this mixture to the coconut purée and cook to 185°F (85°C), checking with a probe thermometer.

3 Beat the mixture with an electric mixer until completely cool. In a separate bowl, whip the chilled cream to soft peaks and gently fold it into the mixture. Refrigerate.

ALMOND COCONUT SPONGE CAKE

4 Place the egg whites, cream of tartar, and sugar in the bowl of a stand mixer and chill in the freezer for 10 minutes.

5 Whip until stiff peaks form. Set aside.

6 In a separate bowl, mix the whole eggs, powdered sugar, and almond flour (do not whip). Stir in the melted butter. Sift in the flour and combine. Gently fold in the whipped egg whites using a rubber spatula.

7 Preheat the oven to 360°F (180°C). Line a baking sheet with parchment paper and place a 12-inch (30-cm) square frame on top. Spread the batter evenly and sprinkle with shredded coconut. Bake for 9 minutes using the convection setting.

8 After baking, place another sheet of parchment on top, flip the sponge cake, and allow to cool.

COCONUT COULIS

9 In a small bowl, bloom gelatin in 3 tbsp of cold water for 5 to 10 minutes.

10 In a medium saucepan, heat the coconut purée and lime zest to 105°F (40°C). Add the gelatin and Malibu rum, blend, and set aside.

ASSEMBLY

11 Flip the cooled sponge cake onto a work surface and remove the parchment. Cut six strips 2 inches (5 cm) tall by 7 ¼ inches (18.5 cm) long. Cut 12 disks with a 1 ¾-inch (4.5 cm) round cutter.

12 Line six 2 ⅓-inch (6-cm) metal rings with acetate strips and place acetate disks at the bottom. (Lining the rings with these flexible plastic strips allows you to unmold your semifreddo easily.)

13 Line the rings with the sponge cake strips and place one disk at the bottom of each mold.

14 Pipe the coconut parfait halfway up each ring. Add a second sponge cake disk to each.

15 Pour about 2 tbsp coconut coulis over each sponge and finish filling with the parfait. Freeze for at least 20 hours.

16 Pipe the remaining parfait into 1 ½-inch (4-cm) silicone dome molds. Freeze for at least 2 hours.

PLATING

17 Unmold the cake-parfaits and remove the acetate strips.

18 Unmold the frozen parfait domes and place one on top of each cake.

19 Use a mandoline to shave coconut and place the curls on each dessert.

CHEF'S TIP

To ensure perfect texture, transfer the desserts to the refrigerator for 15 minutes before serving.

RASPBERRY FROZEN NOUGAT

Prep time: 40 minutes

Cook time: 5 minutes

Freeze time: at least 4 hours

Serves: 8

FROZEN NOUGAT

1 ½ cups (360 ml) heavy cream

⅓ cup (110 g) lavender honey

1 tbsp glucose

3 egg whites

1 tbsp pistachio paste

NUT MIXTURE

⅓ cup (50 g) sliced almonds

¼ cup (40 g) chopped pistachios

¼ cup (40 g) chopped roasted hazelnuts

RASPBERRY COULIS

2 tbsp granulated sugar

2 cups (300 g) fresh raspberries

FOR SERVING

Fresh raspberries, halved

Shiso purple microgreens

FROZEN NOUGAT

1 In a stand mixer, whip the cream to soft peaks and refrigerate.
2 Make an Italian meringue by heating the honey and glucose to 240°F (116°C), then slowly pouring over the egg whites while beating. Continue whipping until stiff peaks form and the meringue has cooled.
3 Loosen the pistachio paste by stirring in 5 tbsp of the whipped cream. Gently fold into the meringue.
4 Fold in the remaining whipped cream using a spatula. Transfer to a piping bag fitted with a plain No. 8 tip. Fill sixteen 2 ⅓-inch (6-cm) silicone half-sphere molds. Freeze for at least 4 hours.

NUT MIXTURE

5 Combine all of the nuts in a shallow bowl.

RASPBERRY COULIS

6 In a saucepan, bring 2 tbsp of water and the sugar to a boil. Add the raspberries and blend using an immersion blender. Strain through a fine mesh sieve. Let cool.

PLATING

7 Unmold the frozen half-spheres and pair them to create full spheres. Roll the spheres in the nut mixture. Return to the freezer.
8 Place each nougat sphere on a plate with a few halved raspberries.
9 Fill the halved raspberries with raspberry coulis using a pipette. Add more coulis to the plate and finish with microgreens.

BEET SOUP WITH GREEN APPLE SORBET

Prep time: 40 minutes

Cook time: 10 minutes

Chill time: 24 hours

Freeze time: 1 hour

Serves: 8

LEMON-GIN GELÉE

¾ cup (150 g) sugar

⅛ tsp agar-agar

1 tsp grated lemon zest

3 tbsp + 1 tsp lemon juice

2 tbsp + 1 tsp The Botanist gin

BEET SOUP

1 ¼ cups (300 ml) beet juice

¼ cup (60 ml) raspberry juice

1 tbsp The Botanist gin

GREEN APPLE SORBET

4 Granny Smith apples

7 tbsp granulated sugar

6 tbsp atomized glucose

1 tsp sorbet stabilizer

3 tbsp lemon juice

CRISPY SPAGHETTI

1 tbsp sesame oil

16 strands spaghetti

1 tbsp wildflower honey

1 tbsp white sesame seeds

FOR SERVING

Atsina cress and purple shiso cress

Edible silver leaf (optional)

LEMON-GIN GELÉE

1 In a saucepan, bring 1 ½ cups (360 ml) of water to a boil. In a small bowl, mix the sugar, agar-agar, and lemon zest together. Whisk the sugar mixture into the boiling water. Add the lemon juice and gin.

2 Quickly pour ⅓ cup (100 g) of the mixture into each of the 8 shallow bowls. Freeze the bowls.

BEET SOUP

3 Mix all the ingredients with 2 tbsp of water and refrigerate.

GREEN APPLE SORBET

4 Peel and core the apples, then purée the flesh until you have 2 cups (500 g).

5 In a saucepan, bring 1 cup and 1 tbsp (255 ml) of water to a boil. Add the sugar, glucose, and stabilizer. Stir and heat the mixture to 212°F (100°C), checking with a probe thermometer.

6 Using an immersion blender, blend the mixture. Transfer to a heatproof container, then cool it quickly in the freezer to 39°F (4°C). Add the apple purée and lemon juice.

7 Let the mixture rest in the refrigerator for 24 hours. Blend again and churn in an ice cream maker.

8 Using a piping bag, fill 40 half-sphere silicone molds, 1 ¼ in (3 cm) in diameter, with the sorbet. Level the surface of each and freeze for at least 1 hour. Unmold, pair them to create full spheres, and return to the freezer.

CRISPY SPAGHETTI

9 In a large pan, heat the sesame oil and lightly toast the spaghetti. Add the honey and bring to a boil, coating the spaghetti. Remove from the pan and roll the toasted spaghetti in sesame seeds.

PLATING

10 Pour 3 tbsp of beet soup over the lemon-gin gelée in the shallow bowls.

11 Arrange 8 sorbet domes, and 2 crispy spaghetti strands. Garnish with small cress leaves and edible silver leaf (optional).

HAZELNUT CHURROS

Prep time: 1 hour 30 minutes

Cook time: 20 minutes

Chill time: 4 hours

Freeze time: 10 minutes after churning

Serves: 8

HAZELNUT ICE CREAM

2 cups (480 ml) whole milk

½ cup (120 ml) heavy cream

1 tbsp + 2 tsp honey

2 tbsp granulated sugar

3 tbsp nonfat dry milk powder

½ tsp ice cream stabilizer

3 egg yolks

½ cup (120 ml) hazelnut praliné

2 tbsp hazelnut paste

TANZANIAN CREAM

1 cup (240 ml) heavy cream

4 egg yolks

¼ cup (50 g) granulated sugar

3 ½ oz (100 g) 75 percent cacao Tanzanian chocolate, chopped

CHURROS

2 ½ tbsp granulated sugar, plus more for coating

¼ cup (60 g) butter

½ tsp salt

1 cup (125 g) all-purpose flour

Zest of 1 orange

Zest of 1 lemon

⅛ tsp ground cinnamon

3 eggs

1 tbsp + 1 tsp orange blossom water

Grapeseed oil, for frying

ISOMALT DECORATION

1 ½ cups (300 g) isomalt

1 tbsp chopped hazelnuts

FOR SERVING

8 glasses for serving

Edible gold leaf (optional)

HAZELNUT ICE CREAM

1 In a saucepan, bring the milk, cream, and honey to a boil.

2 In a mixing bowl, combine the sugar, dry milk, and stabilizer. Add the egg yolks and whisk until the mixture is pale.

3 Pour the egg mixture into the hot liquid and heat everything to 185°F (85°C), checking with a probe thermometer.

4 Stir in the hazelnut praliné and hazelnut paste. Blend with an immersion blender, then cool rapidly to 39°F (4°C) in the freezer.

5 Let infuse in the refrigerator for at least 4 hours. Blend again, then churn in an ice cream maker. Freeze for 10 minutes after churning.

TANZANIAN CREAM

6 In a saucepan, bring the cream to a boil.

7 In a bowl, whisk the egg yolks with the sugar until light in color. Combine with the cream and cook to 185°F (85°C).

8 Strain the hot mixture over the chopped chocolate and blend until smooth. Chill until needed.

CHURROS

9 In a saucepan, combine ½ cup (120 ml) of water, the sugar, butter, and salt. Stir and bring to a boil.

10 Add the flour, orange and lemon zests, and cinnamon. Stir vigorously with a spatula to dry the dough, as you would for pâte à choux.

11 To check if the dough is dry enough, pinch a small bit—it should not be sticky or release moisture.

12 Transfer the dough to a stand mixer fitted with the paddle attachment. Mix while still warm, then add the eggs one at a time. Stir in the orange blossom water. Cover with plastic wrap touching the dough surface and refrigerate.

ISOMALT DECORATION

13 Melt the isomalt in a saucepan. Pour onto a sheet of parchment paper and shape it into 8 rough circles with openings the size of the serving glasses in the center.

14 While still hot, press chopped hazelnuts onto the surface and let it cool.

TO SHAPE AND FRY THE CHURROS

15 Heat the grapeseed oil in a saucepan to between 390 to 410°F (200 to 210°C).

16 Transfer the churro dough to a piping bag fitted with a No. 12 star tip.

17 Once the oil reaches the right temperature, pipe 2- to 2 ½-inch (5- to 6-cm) logs directly into the oil, cutting them with water-dipped scissors.

18 Fry the churros, stirring constantly, until they reach the desired golden color.

19 Remove with a slotted spoon and place on a paper towel. Blot the tops with more paper to absorb the excess oil.

20 Roll the churros in granulated sugar.

PLATING

21 Spoon 2 tbsp of Tanzanian chocolate cream into each serving glass.

22 Add 1 scoop of hazelnut ice cream on top.

23 Place the Isomalt decoration over the ice cream and set 2 churros on top. Finish with a few flecks of edible gold leaf.

CHEF'S TIP

For extra indulgence, fill the churros with chocolate spread. Although similar, praline and praliné are different, this recipe calls for the latter, which is more of a hazelnut paste or powder than a candy.

YUZU CRÊPES SUZETTE

Prep time: 1 hour

Cook time: 10 minutes

Chill time: 4 hours

Freeze time: 10 minutes after churning

Serves: 8

CRÊPE BATTER

6 eggs

2 tbsp granulated sugar

1 tsp orange blossom water

1 tbsp crème fraîche

3 tbsp sunflower oil

½ tsp salt

1 cup (125 g) rice flour

3 tbsp butter, plus more for cooking

2 cups (480 ml) whole milk

YUZU SORBET

1 tbsp orange blossom honey

½ cup (100 g) granulated sugar

⅓ cup (80 g) atomized glucose

1 tsp sorbet stabilizer

1 ¼ cups (300 ml) yuzu juice

ORANGE CARAMEL

1 cup (200 g) granulated sugar

3 tbsp butter

1 cup (240 ml) orange juice

1 tbsp lemon juice

ORANGE SEGMENTS

1 orange

FOR SERVING

Cointreau

Candied orange zest

Purple shiso cress

CRÊPE BATTER

1 In a mixing bowl, whisk together the eggs, sugar, orange blossom water, crème fraîche, sunflower oil, and salt. Add the rice flour and mix until smooth.

2 In a saucepan, melt the butter until it turns golden brown. Pour it into the batter along with 1 ½ cups (360 ml) milk and whisk until fully incorporated. Add more milk if the batter seems too thick.

YUZU SORBET

3 In a saucepan, bring 1 cup (240 ml) of water and the honey to a boil. Stir in the sugar, glucose, and stabilizer. Heat the mixture to 212°F (100°C), checking with a probe thermometer.

4 Blend thoroughly using an immersion blender, then transfer to a heatproof container. Chill quickly in the freezer to 39°F (4°C). Add the yuzu juice and blend again. Refrigerate for 4 hours to infuse.

5 Blend once more before churning in an ice cream maker. Freeze for 10 minutes after churning.

ORANGE CARAMEL

6 In a saucepan, slowly cook the sugar without stirring until it forms a deep amber caramel. Stir in the butter, followed by the orange and lemon juices. Mix until smooth.

ORANGE SEGMENTS

7 Peel the orange with a knife, removing all the white pith. Cut out the segments and set aside.

COOKING THE CRÊPES

8 Grease a skillet and place a 6-inch (16-cm) ring mold inside. Pour in a ladleful of batter and cook over medium heat for 1 minute.

9 Carefully lift off the ring and flip the crêpe to cook the other side.

PLATING

10 Add 2 tbsp of orange caramel to a skillet and place the cooked crêpe in it. Warm gently until the sauce begins to simmer.

11 Fold and transfer the crêpe to a plate. Deglaze the remaining caramel in the skillet with Cointreau and pour the syrup over the crêpe.

12 Garnish with orange segments and candied zest. Add a *quenelle* of yuzu sorbet.

13 Finish with purple shiso cress and small dots of orange caramel

FROZEN CREAM PUFFS

Prep time: 1 hour 30 minutes

Cook time: 30 minutes

Chill time: 24 hours

Freeze time: 1 hour

Serves: 6

TONKA BEAN CUSTARD ICE CREAM

2 ½ cups (600 ml) whole milk

¼ cup (60 g) butter

1 whole tonka bean, grated

⅔ cup (130 g) granulated sugar, divided

⅙ cup (35 g) atomized glucose

½ cup (50 g) skim milk powder

½ tsp ice cream stabilizer

4 egg yolks

CHOUX PASTRY

⅓ cup (80 ml) whole milk

½ tsp salt

½ tsp granulated sugar

3 tbsp butter

½ cup (70 g) all-purpose flour

2 eggs

¼ cup (50 g) pearl sugar

¼ cup (50 g) chopped hazelnuts

YUZU ITALIAN MERINGUE

¾ cup (150 g) granulated sugar

1 tbsp atomized glucose

2 egg whites

⅛ tsp yuzu powder

CARAMEL

2 tbsp glucose

½ cup (90 g) granulated sugar

¼ tsp salt

TONKA BEAN CUSTARD ICE CREAM

1 In a saucepan, bring the milk, butter, and grated tonka bean to a boil. Stir in ½ cup (100 g) of the sugar and the glucose, milk powder, and stabilizer.

2 In a bowl, whisk the egg yolks with the remaining 2 tbsp sugar until pale. Pour into the hot mixture, whisking constantly. Cook to 185°F (85°C), checking with a probe thermometer.

3 Transfer to a heatproof container and cool quickly in the freezer to 39°F (4°C), then refrigerate for 24 hours to allow the flavors to infuse.

4 Strain, blend again, and churn.

CHOUX PASTRY

5 In a saucepan, bring the milk, salt, sugar, and butter to a boil. Remove from the heat, sift in the flour, and stir vigorously. Return to the heat and cook briefly to dry the dough slightly.

6 Transfer the dough to a stand mixer fitted with the paddle attachment. Beat on low for 5 minutes. Add the eggs gradually, mixing well between each.

7 Preheat the oven to 350°F (175°C). Line a baking sheet with parchment paper and pipe the dough using a plain No. 10 tip, about 2 oz (60 g) per puff.

8 Sprinkle the tops with the pearl sugar and chopped hazelnuts. Bake for 27 minutes, using the convection setting.

YUZU ITALIAN MERINGUE

9 In a saucepan, cook the sugar and glucose with ¼ of cup (60 ml) water to 245°F (118°C).

10 Meanwhile, beat the egg whites with an electric mixer to soft peaks. Slowly pour in the hot syrup while mixing. Add the yuzu powder and whip until the mixture cools completely.

CARAMEL

11 In a small saucepan, cook the glucose, sugar, and salt over medium heat without stirring until it turns a deep amber color. Pour into a piping bag while still warm and set aside.

PLATING

12 Cut the cooled cream puffs two-thirds of the way through. Trim the tops neatly using a 1 ½-inch (4-cm) round cutter.

13 Fill each puff with the tonka bean ice cream and add a small dollop of caramel in the center. Freeze until serving time, at least 1 hour.

CHEF'S TIP

When baking the choux, keep the oven door closed during the first phase. Once fully puffed, crack the door slightly to finish drying and achieve a crisp texture.

BAKED ALASKA

Prep time: 1 hour

Cook time: 20 minutes

Chill time: 4 hours

Freeze time: 2 hours

Serves: 8

TROPICAL FRUIT SORBET

⅔ cup (125 g) granulated sugar

⅓ cup (75 g) atomized glucose

1 tsp sorbet stabilizer

⅔ cup (160 ml) mango purée

⅔ cup (160 ml) passion fruit juice

⅔ cup (160 ml) banana purée

⅔ cup (160 ml) orange juice

JOCONDE SPONGE CAKE

1 ¼ cups (125 g) almond flour

1 cup (125 g) powdered sugar

¼ cup (35 g) all-purpose flour

2 tsp acacia honey

3 eggs

2 tbsp butter, melted

3 egg whites

2 tbsp granulated sugar

RUM SYRUP

½ cup (100 g) granulated sugar

3 tbsp + 1 tsp Mount Gay rum

ITALIAN MERINGUE

1 cup (200 g) granulated sugar

1 ½ tbsp atomized glucose

3 egg whites

ASSEMBLY

⅔ cup (160 ml) Mount Gay rum (20 ml per serving)

TROPICAL FRUIT SORBET

1 In a saucepan, bring 1 cup (240 ml) of water to a boil. Add the sugar, glucose, and stabilizer. Heat to 212°F (100°C), checking with a probe thermometer.

2 Stir in the fruit purées and juices, then blend with an immersion blender.

3 Transfer to a heatproof container and chill quickly in the freezer to 39°F (4°C). Refrigerate for at least 4 hours to infuse.

4 Blend again and churn in an ice cream maker.

JOCONDE SPONGE CAKE

5 Preheat the oven to 360°F (180°C).

6 In the bowl of a stand mixer fitted with the paddle attachment, combine the almond flour, powdered sugar, all-purpose flour, honey, and whole eggs. Beat for 10 minutes. Fold in the melted butter.

7 In a separate bowl, whip the egg whites with the granulated sugar with an electric mixer until stiff peaks form. Gently fold into the previous mixture.

8 Spread the batter evenly on a parchment-lined 16-by-24 inch (40-by-60 cm) baking sheet. Bake for 7 minutes on the convection setting.

RUM SYRUP

9 In a saucepan, bring ½ cup (120 ml) of water and the sugar to a boil. Add the rum and stir.

ASSEMBLY

10 Use a 4 ¾-inch (12-cm) round cutter to cut out 8 sponge cake discs.

11 Cut 8 additional discs with a 3-inch (8-cm) cutter.

12 Line eight 3-inch (8-cm) silicone dome molds with the larger sponge cake discs. Soak with rum syrup and freeze for at least 1 hour.

13 Fill a piping bag with tropical fruit sorbet. Pipe into the lined molds and finish by placing the smaller sponge discs on top. Soak with syrup and freeze again for at least 1 hour.

ITALIAN MERINGUE

14 In a saucepan, heat ⅓ cup (80 ml) of water, the sugar, and glucose to 244°F (118°C).

15 In a mixing bowl, beat the egg whites with an electric mixer until foamy. Slowly add in the hot syrup and beat until fully cooled. During cooling, beat the meringue at low speed to prevent it from stiffening too much.

PLATING

16 Dip the frozen domes in the soft Italian meringue.

17 Torch the surface to caramelize lightly and store in the freezer.

18 Before serving, preheat the oven to 360°F (180°C). Place the Baked Alaskas in the oven for 4 minutes.

19 In a small saucepan, heat the rum and ignite. Pour the flaming rum over the Baked Alaska.

CHEF'S TIP

To coat the Baked Alaska with meringue, stick a knife in the base of the frozen dessert and dip it into the very soft meringue.

BACCHUS VACHERIN

Prep time: 1 hour

Cook time: 1 hour 50 minutes

Chill time: 4 hours

Freeze time: 1 hour

Serves: 10

WILD PEACH SORBET

7 tbsp granulated sugar

3 tbsp atomized glucose

1 tsp sorbet stabilizer

2 ½ cups (600 g) wild peach flesh

ROSÉ CHAMPAGNE SORBET

½ cup + 1 tbsp (110 g) granulated sugar

½ cup + 2 tbsp (130 g) atomized glucose

½ tsp sorbet stabilizer

1 ½ cups (360 ml) rosé champagne

SWISS MERINGUE

3 egg whites

1 ⅔ cups (200 g) powdered sugar

DECORATION

Edible silver leaf (optional)

WILD PEACH SORBET

1 In a saucepan, bring ½ cup (120 ml) of water to a boil. Add the sugar, glucose, and stabilizer. Heat to 185°F (85°C), checking with a thermometer.

2 Add the peach flesh, blend with an immersion blender, and transfer to a heatproof container. Chill quickly in the freezer to 39°F (4°C). Infuse in the fridge for 4 hours.

3 Blend again and churn.

ROSÉ CHAMPAGNE SORBET

4 In a saucepan, bring ¾ cup (180 ml) of water to a boil. Add the sugar, glucose, and stabilizer. Heat to 185°F (85°C).

5 Blend with an immersion blender and transfer to a heatproof container. Chill in the freezer to 39°F (4°C), stir in the rosé champagne, and blend again. Refrigerate for 4 hours.

6 Blend once more and churn.

SWISS MERINGUE

7 In a bowl set over a double boiler, whisk together the egg whites and powdered sugar. Heat to 122°F (50°C), whisking constantly.

8 Transfer to a stand mixer and beat until fully cooled.

9 Preheat the oven to 175°F (80°C) using the convection setting. Fill a piping bag fitted with an open star No. 8 tip and pipe spirals onto ten inverted 2 ¾-inch (7-cm) silicone half-dome molds, leaving the center empty to fill with the rosé champagne sorbet.

10 Bake for 1 hour 30 minutes using the convection setting. Let cool slightly, then freeze for 20 minutes.

ASSEMBLY

11 Pipe the wild peach sorbet into ten 2 ¾-inch (7-cm) silicone half-dome molds. Freeze for 30 minutes.

12 Fill the frozen meringue domes with rosé champagne sorbet. Freeze for 20 minutes.

13 Unmold the peach domes and place them over the filled meringue bases.

PLATING

14 Transfer remaining champagne sorbet to a piping bag fitted with a No. 8 tip. Pipe a spiral over the peach dome.

15 Freeze until ready to serve.

16 Garnish each dome with edible silver leaf (optional).

CHEF'S TIP

Swiss meringue holds up much better than French meringue, making it ideal for this kind of dessert.

FROZEN DRINKS

Driven by his passion for flavor and texture, Emmanuel pushes the boundaries of culinary harmony as far as his imagination and technical mastery will take him. In this collection of frozen beverages, textures contrast and complement one another while echoing the interplay of flavors and aromas inspired by his travels.

One standout in these rich and elegant selections is the Coconut Matcha Milkshake—a creamy yet light drink with no acidity, where coconut and matcha blend to create a subtly sweet and intensely flavorful profile. A final flourish of airy matcha foam, which floats like a soft, delicate cloud, lends visual appeal.

Ice cream, which Emmanuel feels is inherently tied to childhood and indulgence, is also at the heart of the Babyccino with Caramelized Marshmallow and Babyccino Ice Cream. Once again drawing on nostalgia, Emmanuel combines hot milk with cold ice cream for a silky mouthfeel, while a caramelized vanilla marshmallow adds sweetness and crunch. This is a simple recipe to make as a family—and it's sure to delight kids and adults alike.

COCONUT MATCHA MILKSHAKE

Prep time: 40 minutes

Cook time: 10 minutes

Chill time: 5 hours

Freeze time: 1 hour

Serves: 6

COCONUT ICE CREAM

1 cup (240 ml) whole milk

⅔ cup (160 ml) heavy cream

⅓ cup (65 g) granulated sugar

2 ½ tbsp atomized glucose

¼ cup (35 g) skim milk powder

½ tsp ice cream stabilizer

¾ cup (180 ml) coconut purée

COCONUT MILKSHAKE

½ cup (120 ml) whole milk

½ cup (125 g) coconut ice cream

2 tsp muscovado sugar

3 tbsp ice cubes

MATCHA SIPHON FOAM

1 cup (240 ml) whole milk

1 cup (240 ml) heavy cream

5 egg yolks

1 tbsp matcha green tea powder

COCONUT ICE CREAM

1 In a saucepan, bring the milk and cream to a boil. Add the sugar, glucose, milk powder, and stabilizer.

2 Stir and heat the mixture to 185°F (85°C), checking with a probe thermometer.

3 Stir in the coconut purée. Using an immersion blender, blend thoroughly. Transfer to a heatproof container and cool quickly in the freezer to 39°F (4°C).

4 Refrigerate for at least 4 hours. Blend again and churn in an ice cream maker.

COCONUT MILKSHAKE

5 Place all ingredients in a blender and mix until smooth.

MATCHA SIPHON FOAM

6 In a saucepan, bring the milk and cream to a boil. Pour over the egg yolks in a separate bowl, whisking constantly. Return to the heat and cook to 185°F (85°C), stirring continuously.

7 Add the matcha powder and blend. Cool quickly in the freezer y to 39°F (4°C), then refrigerate.

8 Once chilled, pour the mixture into a siphon. Charge with one gas cartridge and refrigerate for at least 1 hour.

PLATING

9 Fill each glass three-quarters of the way with the coconut milkshake. Top with a generous swirl of matcha foam from the siphon.

CHEF'S TIP

For best results, charge the siphon with the matcha foam and gas cartridge at least 3 hours ahead of time and keep it refrigerated. Shake gently before using. The foam should be smooth, glossy, and hold its shape. If it doesn't, shake the siphon again, vertically, with the nozzle pointing down.

BABYCCINO WITH CARAMELIZED MARSHMALLOW AND BABYCCINO ICE CREAM

Prep time: 1 hour

Cook time: 20 minutes

Chill time: 4 hours

Serves: 5

BABYCCINO ICE CREAM

2 cups (480 ml) whole milk

⅔ cup (160 ml) heavy cream

½ cup (90 g) granulated sugar

¼ cup (50 g) atomized glucose

3 tbsp skim milk powder

¾ tsp ice cream stabilizer

⅓ cup (80 ml) sweetened condensed milk

VANILLA WHITE HOT CHOCOLATE

1 cup (240 ml) whole milk

1 cup (240 ml) heavy cream

½ tsp vanilla powder

¾ cup (150 g) white chocolate, chopped

VANILLA MARSHMALLOW

3 ½ tsp powdered gelatin

1 egg white

1 cup (220 g) granulated sugar

2 tbsp glucose syrup

1 tsp vanilla powder

neutral oil, for greasing

¾ cup (100 g) powdered sugar

¾ cup (100 g) cornstarch

MILK FOAM

1 ¼ cups (300 ml) whole milk

FOR SERVING

4 to 5 dried vanilla bean halves

BABYCCINO ICE CREAM

1 In a saucepan, bring the milk and cream to a boil. Add the sugar, glucose, milk powder, and stabilizer.

2 Stir thoroughly and cook to 185°F (85°C), checking with a probe thermometer.

3 Add the sweetened condensed milk and blend. Cool quickly in the freezer to 39°F (4°C).

4 Refrigerate for 4 hours.

5 Blend again and churn.

VANILLA WHITE HOT CHOCOLATE

6 In a saucepan, bring the milk, cream, and vanilla powder to a boil. Remove from the heat, add the chocolate, and whisk until fully melted. Blend with an immersion blender.

VANILLA MARSHMALLOW

7 In a small bowl, bloom the gelatin in 5 to 6 tbsp of cold water for 5 to 10 minutes.

8 In a stand mixer, whip the egg white until frothy.

9 In a saucepan, heat the sugar, glucose, and 5 tbsp of water to 257°F (125°C) using a candy thermometer. Stir bloomed gelatin into the syrup.

10 Pour the syrup into the egg white while beating. Whip until the mixture is just warm. Add the vanilla powder and mix well.

11 Transfer the marshmallow mixture to a piping bag fitted with a plain No. 6 tip.

12 Lightly grease silicone pebble molds with neutral oil and pipe in the marshmallow. Let sit at room temperature for at least 2 hours.

13 Meanwhile, sift the powdered sugar and cornstarch together. Unmold the marshmallows and coat them in the mixture. Store in a dry place.

MILK FOAM

14 Heat the milk in a saucepan to 140°F (60°C). Froth using an immersion blender until foamy.

PLATING

15 Pour ½ cup (120 ml) of vanilla white hot chocolate into 5 shallow bowls.

16 Lightly toast 15 marshmallows with a kitchen torch. Add 3 lightly caramelized marshmallows to each bowl.

17 Add a scoop of Babyccino ice cream and spoon milk foam on top of each.

18 Garnish with the half dried vanilla beans.

CHEF'S TIP

This dessert is a real crowd-pleaser for kids—rich, comforting, and indulgent. My daughter Marie-Lou absolutely loves it.

VIENNESE HOT CHOCOLATE WITH HAZELNUT PRALINÉ ICE CREAM

Prep time: 45 minutes

Cook time: 20 minutes

Chill time: 4 hours

Freeze time: 10 minutes after churning

Serves: 4

HAZELNUT PRALINÉ

1 cup (200 g) granulated sugar

1 ⅓ cups (200 g) hazelnuts, toasted

HAZELNUT PRALINÉ ICE CREAM

2 ½ cups (600 ml) whole milk

¼ cup (60 g) butter

⅔ cup (130 g) granulated sugar

¼ cup (35 g) atomized glucose

⅓ cup (50 g) skim milk powder

½ tsp ice cream stabilizer

4 egg yolks

Hazelnut praliné (recipe following)

VANILLA WHIPPED CREAM

1 vanilla bean

¾ cup (180 ml) heavy cream, cold

1 tbsp powdered sugar

INTENSE HOT CHOCOLATE

⅔ cup (160 ml) whole milk

⅔ cup (160 ml) heavy cream

1 tsp vanilla powder

1 tbsp cocoa powder

1 tsp granulated sugar

⅛ tsp ground cinnamon

5 ¼ oz (150 g) 75 percent cacao Tanzanian chocolate, chopped

HAZELNUT PRALINÉ

1 In a saucepan, heat the sugar with 3 tbsp of water until it forms a caramel. Add the toasted hazelnuts and stir to coat.

2 Transfer the caramelized hazelnuts onto a sheet of parchment paper. Let cool.

3 Once cooled, crush and blend into a coarse powder using a food processor. Set aside.

HAZELNUT PRALINÉ ICE CREAM

4 In a saucepan, bring the milk and butter to a boil.

5 In a bowl, combine the sugar, glucose, milk powder, and stabilizer.

6 In another bowl, whisk the egg yolks with half of the dry mixture until pale.

7 Pour the hot milk over the yolk mixture while whisking. Stir in the remaining dry ingredients.

8 Return the mixture to the saucepan and heat gently to 185°F (85°C), checking with a probe thermometer.

9 Blend using an immersion blender, then transfer to a heatproof container. Cool quickly in the freezer to 39°F (4°C).

10 Refrigerate for 4 hours to infuse.

11 Blend again and churn. After churning, gently fold in the hazelnut praliné powder using a spatula. Freeze for 10 minutes.

VANILLA WHIPPED CREAM

12 Place a mixing bowl and beaters in the freezer.

13 Split the vanilla bean and scrape out the seeds with a knife.

14 In the chilled bowl, combine the cream, vanilla seeds, and powdered sugar. Whip to soft peaks. Refrigerate until ready to use.

INTENSE HOT CHOCOLATE

15 In a saucepan, combine the milk, cream, vanilla, cocoa, sugar, and cinnamon. Bring to a boil while whisking, then remove from the heat.

16 Add the chopped chocolate. Stir to melt, then blend with an immersion blender.

PLATING

17 In a shallow bowl or mug, spoon in the vanilla whipped cream. Add a scoop of hazelnut praliné ice cream. Pour in the hot chocolate just before serving.

FROZEN MACARONS

These delicate almond meringue shells, crisp on the outside and tender inside, become even more irresistible when filled with smooth, frozen cream. Here, Emmanuel pairs the shells with a variety of ice creams and sorbets to create elegant treats perfect for ending a meal or enjoying as an indulgent snack. Note: The recipes call for "macaroning" the batter; this is the lengthy but important process of folding dry ingredients into meringue until the batter eventually falls like ribbons from the spatula.

Macarons are notoriously finicky and the amount of air each individual whips into their meringue may vary, which creates differences in the volume. Because of that, we recommend using the weight measurements to ensure accuracy.

CHOCOLATE MACARONS WITH MILK CHOCOLATE COMBAVA ICE CREAM

Prep time: 1 hour 30 minutes

Cook time: 20 minutes

Chill time: 4 hours

Rest time: 30 minutes

Freeze time: 10 minutes after churning

Makes: 30 mini macarons

MILK CHOCOLATE COMBAVA ICE CREAM

2 cups (480 ml) whole milk

½ cup (120 ml) heavy cream

2 tsp acacia honey

1 tsp grated combava zest

⅓ cup (80 g) granulated sugar, divided

¼ cup (30 g) skim milk powder

¾ tsp ice cream stabilizer

1 egg yolk

5 ¼ oz (150 g) 36 percent cacao milk chocolate, chopped

ITALIAN MACARON MERINGUE

¾ cup (160 g) granulated sugar

¼ tsp salt

2 egg whites

CHOCOLATE MACARON BATTER

1 ½ oz (40 g) 100 percent cacao dark chocolate

1 cup (115 g) almond flour

1 cup (115 g) powdered sugar

2 egg whites

1 tbsp cocoa powder

2 generous cups (200 g) Italian macaron meringue (recipe following)

MILK CHOCOLATE COMBAVA ICE CREAM

1 In a saucepan, combine the milk, cream, honey, and combava zest. Bring to a boil. Add ¼ cup (50 g) of the sugar, the milk powder, and stabilizer. Mix well.

2 In a bowl, whisk the egg yolk with the remaining sugar. Gradually add to the hot mixture while whisking. Cook to 185°F (85°C) checking with a probe thermometer.

3 Remove from the heat and add the milk chocolate, stirring until melted. Blend using an immersion blender and strain through a fine sieve to remove the zest. Transfer to a heatproof container and cool quickly in the freezer to 39°F (4°C).

4 Refrigerate for at least 4 hours.

5 Blend again and churn. Freeze for 10 minutes after churning.

ITALIAN MACARON MERINGUE

6 In a saucepan, heat 3 tbsp of water, the sugar, and salt to 240°F (116°C).

7 Lightly whip the egg whites until foamy. Slowly pour in the hot syrup and beat for about 1 minute more.

CHOCOLATE MACARON BATTER

8 In a saucepan, melt the chocolate to 113°F (45°C).

9 In a stand mixer, blend the almond flour with the powdered sugar. Blend in the egg whites, melted chocolate, and cocoa powder. Mix until smooth. Fold in the Italian macaron meringue by hand.

10 Macaron the batter by smoothing and folding it gently with a spatula until it flows evenly, without overworking.

PIPING THE MACARONS

11 Preheat the oven to 295°F (145°C) using the convection setting.

12 Transfer the batter to a piping bag fitted with a plain No. 8 tip.

13 Pipe small rounds onto a baking sheet lined with parchment. Tap the tray to flatten slightly. Let rest at room temperature for about 30 minutes.

14 Bake for 10 to 13 minutes. Let cool.

ASSEMBLY

15 Flip half the macaron shells and place the tray in the freezer for 5 minutes.

16 Using a piping bag, fill the flipped shells with chocolate combava ice cream. Top with the remaining, unflipped shells and freeze until ready to serve.

CHEF'S TIP

You can substitute lime zest for combava (also known as makrut lime) in equal weight, but combava adds a truly unique citrusy depth to this recipe.

TURMERIC MACARONS WITH MANGO SORBET

Prep time: 1 hour 30 minutes

Cook time: 20 minutes

Chill time: 4 hours

Rest time: 30 minutes

Freeze time: 10 minutes after churning

Makes: 30 mini macarons

MANGO SORBET

¾ cup (160 g) granulated sugar

⅓ cup (80 g) atomized glucose

½ tsp sorbet stabilizer

2 ½ cups (600 g) mango flesh

ITALIAN MACARON MERINGUE

⅔ cup (130 g) granulated sugar

¼ tsp salt

1 egg white

TURMERIC MACARON BATTER

½ tsp turmeric

1 cup (125 g) almond flour

1 cup (125 g) powdered sugar

1 egg white

1 ⅔ generous cups (160 g) Italian macaron meringue (recipe following)

MANGO SORBET

1 In a saucepan, bring ⅔ cup (160 ml) of water to a boil. Add the sugar, glucose, and stabilizer. Heat the mixture to 185°F (85°C) checking with a probe thermometer.

2 Add the mango and blend using an immersion blender. Transfer to a heatproof container and cool quickly in the freezer to 39°F (4°C).

3 Refrigerate for at least 4 hours to infuse.

4 Blend again and churn in an ice cream maker. Freeze for 10 minutes after churning.

ITALIAN MACARON MERINGUE

5 In a saucepan, heat 3 tbsp of water, the sugar, and salt to 240°F (116°C).

6 Lightly whip the egg white until frothy. Slowly pour the syrup over the egg white and beat for about 1 minute.

TURMERIC MACARON BATTER

7 Mix the turmeric with 1 ½ tsp of water.

8 In a stand mixer, blend the almond flour and powdered sugar. Blend in the egg white and turmeric mixture. Fold the Italian meringue by hand.

9 Macaron the batter by smoothing and folding it gently with a spatula until it flows evenly, without overworking.

PIPING THE MACARONS

10 Transfer the batter to a piping bag fitted with a plain No. 8 tip.

11 Pipe evenly spaced rounds onto a baking sheet lined with parchment. Tap the tray to flatten slightly. Let rest for about 30 minutes at room temperature.

12 Preheat the oven to 295°F (145°C) on the convection setting and bake for 10 to 13 minutes. Let cool completely.

ASSEMBLY

13 Flip half the macaron shells and place the tray in the freezer for 5 minutes.

14 Using a piping bag, fill the flipped shells with mango sorbet. Top with the remaining, unflipped shells and store in the freezer until ready to serve.

CHEF'S TIP

To avoid using food coloring, I achieve a beautiful yellow shade with ground turmeric or juice. I love the taste of turmeric, which I discovered during a trip to Malaysia.

ORANGE BLOSSOM MACARONS WITH PISTACHIO ICE CREAM

Prep time: 1 hour 30 minutes

Cook time: 20 minutes

Chill time: 4 hours

Rest time: 30 minutes

Freeze time: 10 minutes after churning

Makes: 30 mini macarons

PISTACHIO ICE CREAM

2 cups (240 ml) whole milk

½ cup (120 ml) heavy cream

¼ cup (60 ml) inverted sugar

¼ cup (50 g) granulated sugar, divided

2 ½ tbsp atomized glucose

¼ cup (35 g) skim milk powder

¾ tsp ice cream stabilizer

3 egg yolks

¼ cup (50 g) pistachio paste

ITALIAN MACARON MERINGUE

⅔ cup (130 g) granulated sugar

¼ tsp salt

1 egg white

ORANGE BLOSSOM MACARON BATTER

1 cup (125 g) almond flour

1 cup (125 g) powdered sugar

1 egg white

1 tsp orange blossom water

1 ⅓ generous cups (150 g) Italian macaron meringue (recipe following)

Chopped pistachios, for garnish

PISTACHIO ICE CREAM

1. In a saucepan, combine the milk, cream, and inverted sugar. Bring to a boil. Add 2 tbsp granulated sugar, glucose, milk powder, and stabilizer. Stir well.
2. In a bowl, whisk the egg yolks with the remaining 2 tbsp sugar. Pour into the hot mixture while whisking. Cook to 185°F (85°C) checking with a probe thermometer.
3. Add the pistachio paste and, using an immersion blender, blend thoroughly. Transfer to a heatproof container and cool quickly in the freezer to 39°F (4°C).
4. Refrigerate for at least 4 hours to infuse.
5. Blend again and churn in an ice cream maker. Freeze for 10 minutes after churning.

ITALIAN MACARON MERINGUE

6. In a saucepan, heat 3 tbsp of water, the sugar, and salt to 240°F (116°C).
7. Lightly whip the egg white until foamy. Slowly pour in the syrup and beat for about 1 minute.

ORANGE BLOSSOM MACARON BATTER

8. In a stand mixer, blend the almond flour and powdered sugar. Blend in the egg white and orange blossom water. Fold in the Italian meringue by hand.
9. Macaron the batter by smoothing and folding it gently with a spatula until it flows evenly, without overworking.

PIPING THE MACARONS

10. Transfer the batter to a piping bag fitted with a plain No. 8 tip.
11. Pipe evenly spaced rounds onto a baking sheet lined with parchment. Tap the tray to flatten slightly. Sprinkle chopped pistachios over the tops. Let rest for 30 minutes at room temperature.
12. Preheat the oven to 295°F (145°C) using the convection setting and bake for 10 to 13 minutes. Let cool completely.

ASSEMBLY

13. Flip half the macaron shells and place the tray in the freezer for 5 minutes.
14. Using a piping bag, fill the flipped shells with pistachio ice cream. Top with the remaining, unflipped shells and store in the freezer until ready to serve.

CHOCOLATE MACARONS WITH FRESH MINT ICE CREAM

Prep time: 2 hours

Cook time: 20 minutes

Chill time: 4 hours

Rest time: 30 minutes

Freeze time: 10 minutes after churning

Makes: 70 mini macarons

FRESH MINT ICE CREAM

2 cups (480 ml) whole milk

1 ½ oz (40 g) mint leaves

⅔ cup (160 ml) heavy cream

½ cup (120 g) granulated sugar

¼ cup (50 g) atomized glucose

¼ cup (50 g) skim milk powder

¾ tsp ice cream stabilizer

ITALIAN MACARON MERINGUE

1 ⅔ cups (320 g) granulated sugar

½ tsp salt

3 egg whites

CHOCOLATE MACARON BATTER

1 ½ oz (40 g) 100 percent cacao dark chocolate, chopped

1 cup (115 g) almond flour

1 cup (115 g) powdered sugar

2 egg whites

1 tbsp cocoa powder

2 generous cups (200 g) Italian macaron meringue (recipe following)

MINT MACARON BATTER

1 cup (125 g) almond flour

1 cup (125 g) powdered sugar

1 egg white

6 drops mint extract, such as Ricqlès

3 drops pistachio green food coloring

1 drop lemon yellow food coloring

1 ⅔ cups (150 g) Italian macaron meringue (recipe following)

FRESH MINT ICE CREAM

1 In a blender, combine the milk with the mint leaves and blend. Then strain through a fine sieve.

2 In a saucepan, bring the infused milk and cream to a boil. Add the sugar, glucose, milk powder, and stabilizer. Stir well and heat to 185°F (85°C) checking with a probe thermometer.

3 Blend using an immersion blender, transfer to a heatproof container, and cool quickly in the freezer to 39°F (4°C).

4 Refrigerate for at least 4 hours to infuse.

5 Blend again and churn in an ice cream maker. Freeze for 10 minutes after churning.

ITALIAN MACARON MERINGUE

6 In a saucepan, heat ⅓ cup (80 ml) of water, the sugar, and salt to 240°F (116°C).

7 Lightly whip the egg whites in a mixing bowl. Slowly pour in the hot syrup and beat for 1 more minute.

CHOCOLATE MACARON BATTER

8 In a saucepan, gently melt the chocolate to 113°F (45°C), then remove from the heat.

9 In a stand mixer, blend the almond flour and powdered sugar. Blend in the egg whites, melted chocolate, and cocoa powder. Fold in the Italian meringue by hand.

10 Macaron the batter by smoothing and folding it gently with a spatula until it flows evenly, without overworking.

MINT MACARON BATTER

11 In a stand mixer, blend the almond flour and powdered sugar. Blend in the egg white, mint extract, and food colorings. Fold in the Italian meringue by hand.

12 Macaron the batter by smoothing and folding it gently with a spatula until it flows evenly, without overworking.

PIPING THE MACARONS

13 Transfer the chocolate batter to a piping bag fitted with a plain No. 8 tip.

14 Transfer the mint batter to a piping bag fitted with a plain No. 6 tip.

15 Pipe the chocolate macarons onto a parchment-lined baking sheet, leaving space between each. Immediately pipe a drop of mint batter into the center of each chocolate disc. Tap the tray to level the surface. Let rest for 30 minutes at room temperature.

16 Preheat the oven to 295°F (145°C) using the convection setting and bake for 10 to 13 minutes. Let cool.

ASSEMBLY

17 Flip half the macaron shells and place the tray in the freezer for 5 minutes.

18 Using a piping bag, fill the flipped shells with the mint ice cream. Top with the remaining, unflipped shells. Freeze until ready to serve.

CHEF'S TIP

I first created this bicolored macaron in 2006 for the famous Café Pouchkine. You must pipe the second batter quickly over the first, before it begins to form a skin. Otherwise, the two layers will separate during baking.

MATCHA MACARONS WITH GREEN TEA SORBET

Prep time: 1 hour 30 minutes

Cook time: 20 minutes

Chill time: 4 hours

Rest time: 30 minutes

Freeze time: 10 minutes after churning

Makes: 30 mini macarons

GREEN TEA SORBET

1 tbsp chestnut honey

¼ cup (50 g) granulated sugar

⅔ cup (140 g) atomized glucose

¾ tsp sorbet stabilizer

1 tbsp matcha green tea powder

ITALIAN MACARON MERINGUE

⅔ cup (130 g) granulated sugar

¼ tsp salt

1 egg white

MATCHA MACARON BATTER

1 tbsp matcha green tea powder

1 cup (120 g) almond flour

1 cup (120 g) powdered sugar

1 egg white

1 ⅔ generous cups (155 g) macaron meringue (recipe following)

GREEN TEA SORBET

1 In a saucepan, bring 2 cups (480 ml) of water and the honey to a boil. Add the sugar, glucose, and stabilizer. Stir and heat to 185°F (85°C), checking with a probe thermometer.

2 Stir in the matcha powder and blend with an immersion blender. Transfer to a heatproof container and cool quickly in the freezer to 39°F (4°C).

3 Refrigerate for at least 4 hours to infuse.

4 Blend again and churn in an ice cream maker. Freeze for 10 minutes after churning.

ITALIAN MACARON MERINGUE

5 In a saucepan, heat 3 tbsp of water, the sugar, and salt to 240°F (116°C).

6 Lightly whip the egg white in a bowl. Slowly pour in the hot syrup and beat for 1 minute.

MATCHA MACARON BATTER

7 In a small bowl, mix 1 ½ tbsp of water with the matcha powder until dissolved.

8 In a stand mixer, blend the almond flour and powdered sugar. Blend in the egg white and matcha mixture. Fold in the Italian meringue by hand.

9 Macaron the batter by smoothing and folding it gently with a spatula until it flows evenly, without overworking.

PIPING THE MACARONS

10 Transfer the batter to a piping bag fitted with a plain No. 8 tip.

11 Pipe rounds onto a parchment-lined baking sheet, leaving some space in between. Tap the tray to release air bubbles. Let rest for 30 minutes at room temperature.

12 Preheat the oven to 295°F (145°C) using the convection setting and bake for 10 to 13 minutes. Let cool completely.

ASSEMBLY

13 Flip half the macaron shells and place the tray in the freezer for 5 minutes.

14 Using a piping bag, fill the flipped sides with green tea sorbet. Top with the remaining, unflipped shells. Freeze until ready to serve.

VANILLA MACARONS WITH OKINAWAN BLACK SUGAR ICE CREAM

Prep time: 1 hour 30 minutes

Cook time: 20 minutes

Chill time: 4 hours

Rest time: 30 minutes

Freeze time: 10 minutes after churning

Makes: 30 mini macarons

OKINAWAN BLACK SUGAR ICE CREAM

2 cups (480 ml) whole milk

¾ cup (180 ml) heavy cream

⅔ cup (140 g) Okinawan black sugar, divided

⅓ cup (40 g) skim milk powder

⅙ cup (35 g) atomized glucose

¾ tsp ice cream stabilizer

2 egg yolks

ITALIAN MACARON MERINGUE

⅔ cup (130 g) granulated sugar

¼ tsp salt

1 egg white

VANILLA MACARON BATTER

1 cup (125 g) almond flour

1 cup (125 g) powdered sugar

1 egg white

¾ tsp vanilla extract

1 ⅓ generous cups (160 g) macaron Italian meringue

Vanilla powder, for dusting

OKINAWAN BLACK SUGAR ICE CREAM

1 In a saucepan, combine the milk and cream. Bring to a boil. Add ½ cup (110 g) of the black sugar, milk powder, glucose, and stabilizer. Stir well.

2 In a mixing bowl, whisk the egg yolks with the remaining black sugar. Add the hot liquid gradually while whisking, then return everything to the saucepan. Cook to 185°F (85°C), checking with a probe thermometer.

3 Blend thoroughly using an immersion blender, and transfer to a heatproof container. Cool quickly in the freezer to 39°F (4°C).

4 Refrigerate for at least 4 hours.

5 Blend again and churn in an ice cream maker. Freeze for 10 minutes after churning.

ITALIAN MACARON MERINGUE

6 In a saucepan, heat 3 tbsp of water, the sugar, and salt to 240°F (116°C).

7 Lightly whip the egg white in a bowl. Slowly pour in the hot syrup and beat for 1 minute.

VANILLA MACARON BATTER

8 In a stand mixer, blend the almond flour and powdered sugar. Blend in the egg white and vanilla. Fold in the Italian meringue by hand.

9 Macaron the batter by smoothing and folding it gently with a spatula until it flows evenly, without overworking.

PIPING THE MACARONS

10 Transfer the batter to a piping bag fitted with a plain No. 8 tip.

11 Pipe evenly spaced rounds onto a parchment-lined baking sheet. Tap the tray to level. Dust lightly with vanilla powder. Let rest for 30 minutes at room temperature.

12 Preheat the oven to 295°F (145°C) using the convection setting. Bake for 10 to 13 minutes. Let cool.

ASSEMBLY

13 Flip half the macaron shells and place the tray in the freezer for 5 minutes.

14 Using a piping bag, fill the flipped shells with black sugar ice cream. Top with the remaining, unflipped shells. Freeze until ready to serve.

CHEF'S TIP

I discovered Okinawan black sugar on my many trips to Japan and find its complex flavor unparalleled. If you can't find it online, you can substitute muscovado sugar or galabé sugar from Réunion Island.

APPENDICES

BASE RECIPE: CLASSIC CONE

Prep time: 30 minutes

Rest time: 1 hour

Cook time: About 2 minutes (depends on waffle iron)

Makes: 10 cones

1 egg

½ cup (100 g) granulated sugar

2 ½ cups (300 g) all-purpose flour

⅔ cup (160 ml) whole milk

1 tsp vanilla powder

7 tbsp butter, melted

1. In a bowl, whisk together the egg and sugar. Add the flour and mix.
2. Gradually incorporate the milk, ⅔ cup (160 ml) of water, vanilla powder, and finally the melted butter.
3. Refrigerate for 1 hour.
4. Preheat the cone waffle iron for 5 minutes.
5. Ladle enough batter to cover the iron, close the top, and cook.
6. Carefully remove the cone from the iron and immediately shape around a cone mold. It only takes a couple of minutes for each cone to cool and hold its shape.

BASE RECIPE: CHOCOLATE CONE

Prep time: 30 minutes

Rest time: 1 hour

Cook time: About 2 minutes (depends on waffle iron)

Makes: 15 cones

½ cup (100 g) crème fraîche

½ cup (100 g) granulated sugar

1 egg white

½ cup (70 g) all-purpose flour

2 tbsp cocoa powder

2 tbsp chestnut honey

Pinch of salt

1. In a medium bowl, mix all the ingredients until smooth and homogeneous.
2. Refrigerate for 1 hour.
3. Preheat the cone waffle iron for 5 minutes.
4. Ladle enough batter to cover the iron, close the top, and cook.
5. Carefully remove the cone from the iron and immediately shape around a cone mold. It only takes a couple of minutes for each cone to cool and hold its shape.

CHEF'S TIP

If you don't have a cone mold, you can easily make one using flexible cardboard. Wrap the cooked cone inside your homemade mold and let it cool in shape.

TABLE OF CONTENTS

POPSICLES, GRANITAS, AND FROZEN YOGURTS

FROZEN DESSERTS

FROZEN DRINKS

FROZEN MACARONS

INGREDIENTS INDEX

ACKNOWLEDGMENTS

This book was born from an encounter with two wonderful people, Delphine, the photographer, and Mélanie, the stylist. They came to me with a book project about the worldof ice cream and sorbets, with a very feminine vision. They convinced me in less than a minute.

Laure Aline and her team at Éditions de La Martinière also made this beautiful project possible.

I would also like to highlight the wonderful work of Benjamin, who, with his graphic designer's eye, was able to give a unifying theme to my creations in this book.

Bravo and thank you to everyone!

A big thank you to my daughter Marie-Lou and to Virginie.

A huge thank you to my parents, who encouraged me in my career choice.

I wish everyone had parents like mine.

The Art of Frozen Desserts
By Emmanuel Ryon

Text, photography and styling:
Emmanuel Ryon, Mélanie Martin and Delphine Constantini

U.S. Edition Publisher & Creative Director
Ilona Oppenheim

U.S. Edition Editor
Amanda Faison

U.S. Edition Art Director and Cover Design
Jefferson Quintana

U.S. Edition Editorial Director
Lisa McGuinness

U.S. Edition Publishing Director
Jessica Faroy

U.S. Edition Senior Designer
Morgane Leoni

Printed and bound in China by Artron Art Co., Ltd.

First published in France under the title:
Givré. L'art de la pâtisserie glacée en 60 recettes

The Art of Frozen Desserts was first published in the United States by Tra Publishing, 2026.

ISBN: 978-1-9620983-8-0

This product is made of FSC® -certified and other controlled material.

Tra Publishing is committed to sustainability in its materials and practices.

Tra Publishing
245 NE 37th Street
Miami, FL 33137
trapublishing.com

T tra.publishing

1 2 3 4 5 6 7 8 9 10